CAKES
BISCUITS
BREADS

366
RECIPES

CAKES
BISCUITS
BREADS

SUNBURST BOOKS

ISBN 1 85778 054 X

Printed and bound in India

CONTENTS

Family Cakes *6*

Sponge Cakes *23*

Small Cakes *46*

Scones *60*

Pastries *69*

Biscuits *89*

Tea Breads *151*

Savoury Breads *173*

Cheesecakes and Gateaux *183*

Index *189*

FAMILY CAKES

PINEAPPLE CAKE
Makes a 7 inch (18 cm) cake

14 oz (400 g) can crushed pineapple
6 oz (175 g) butter or soft margarine
6 oz (175 g) caster sugar
3 eggs, beaten

10 oz (275 g) self-raising flour, sifted
2 level tsp baking powder
¼ level tsp mixed spice
2 oz (50 g) ground almonds

Preheat the oven to 350°F/180°C/Gas Mk 4. Grease and line a 7 inch (18 cm) square cake tin. Drain the juice from the can of pineapple and reserve. Roughly chop the fruit, keeping about eight good pieces of fruit for decoration. Place the butter or margarine, sugar, eggs and 3 tbsp juice in a mixing bowl. Sift in the flour, mixed spice and baking powder and stir well. Add the ground almonds and chopped pineapple pieces. Beat all the ingredients together for 2-3 minutes. Spoon into the tin, smooth over the top and place the eight pieces of pineapple around the edge. Bake in the centre of the oven for 1¼-1½ hours until golden brown and firm to the touch. Leave in the cake tin for a few minutes and then carefully turn out onto a wire rack. Remove the greaseproof paper and leave to cool.

ALMOND AND CHERRY CAKE WITH SHERRY
Makes a 7 inch (18 cm) round cake

4 oz (110 g) flour
4 oz (110 g) self-raising flour
pinch of salt
9 oz (250 g) glacé cherries,
  washed and halved

6 oz (175 g) butter
6 oz (175 g) caster sugar
3 medium eggs, lightly beaten
3 oz (75g) ground almonds
6 tbsp sweet sherry

Preheat the oven to 350°F/180°C/Gas Mk 4. Grease and line a 7 inch (18 cm) deep round cake tin. Sift the flours and salt together in a bowl. Toss the cherries in 3 tbsp of the flour. Cream the butter in a large mixing bowl, add the sugar and beat until light and fluffy. Add the eggs gradually and beat well. Fold in the flour and almonds with a metal spoon until thoroughly mixed with the rest of the ingredients. Mix in the sherry and fold in the cherries. Place mixture into the cake tin and bake in the oven for 1¼ hours or until cake has shrunk slightly from the sides of the container. Remove from oven and leave cake in tin for 15 minutes. Turn out and cool on a wire rack.

SEED CAKE
Makes a 7 inch (18 cm) cake

6 oz (175 g) margarine	8 oz (225 g) plain flour
6 oz (175 g) caster sugar	1½ level tsp baking powder
3 standard eggs	8 oz (225 g) plain flour
2 rounded tsp caraway seeds	2 tbsp milk

Preheat the oven to 325°F/170°C/Gas Mk 3. Brush a deep round 7 inch (18 cm) cake tin with melted fat. Line base and side with greaseproof paper and brush lightly with oil or melted fat. Cream margarine and sugar together until light and fluffy. Beat the eggs together and add gradually, beating well after each addition. Stir in the caraway seeds. Sift flour and baking powder together and fold into creamed mixture, alternating with the milk, cutting through the mixture with a metal spoon. Spread mixture evenly in tin and level top with the back of a spoon. Bake in centre of oven for 1¼ to 1½ hours. Test by pressing with fingers. If cooked, cake should spring back, have stopped bubbling and have begun to shrink from side of tin. Leave to cool in the tin for 5-10 minutes. Turn out, remove paper and leave to cool on a wire rack.

JACK HORNER CAKE
Makes an 8 inch (20 cm) cake

8 oz (225 g) butter or margarine	1 tsp baking powder
8 oz (225 g) caster sugar	10 large ripe plums, halved and stoned
4 eggs, beaten	1 tbsp soft light brown sugar
½ tsp vanilla essence	caster sugar for decoration
8 oz (225 g) self-raising flour, sifted	

Preheat the oven to 350°F/180°C/Gas Mk 4. Put the butter, sugar, eggs and vanilla essence in a food processor. Sift in the flour and baking powder and beat for 30-60 seconds until smooth and glossy. If a food processor is not available, the mix can be beaten with an electric mixer for 1-2 minutes, or it can be made in the usual way by creaming fat and sugar together, beating in the eggs and vanilla essence and finally folding in the flour. Chop five of the plums and fold into the cake mixture. Spoon into a lightly greased, lined 8 inch (20 cm) round cake tin and level the surface. Arrange the remaining plum halves on top and sprinkle with the brown sugar. Bake in the centre of the oven for 1¼-1½ hours or until a skewer inserted into the cake comes out clean. Leave to cool in the tin and then remove and peel off the lining paper. Sprinkle caster sugar on top of the cake before serving.

RICH FRUIT CAKE
Makes an 8 inch (20 cm) deep round cake

10 oz (275 g) dates
10 oz (275 g) butter or margarine
8 oz (225 g) caster sugar
6 eggs
1 orange and 1 lemon, peeled,
  deseeded and liquidised

10 oz (275 g) self-raising flour, sifted
1½ lb (675 g) currants
2 tsp mixed spice
1 tsp ginger
1 tsp sea salt
6 oz (175 g) ground almonds

Soak dates overnight in a little water then liquidise. Grease and line an 8 in (20 cm) deep cake tin. Preheat the oven to 300°F/150°C/Gas Mk 2. Cream butter and sugar until light and fluffy, mix with dates. Whisk in one egg at a time. (add a little sifted flour between eggs if mixture starts to curdle). Add liquidised orange and lemon, and mix well. Sift in half the flour, fold in then add dried fruit, spices, salt and almonds alternately with the remaining flour into the creamed mixture. Bake for about 3½ hours or until an skewer comes out cleanly. Cool for 10-15 minutes in the tin before turning out on to a wire rack.

GUINNESS CAKE
Makes an 8 inch (20 cm) round cake

8 oz (225 g) butter
8 oz (225 g) soft brown sugar
4 eggs, lightly beaten
10 oz (275 g) plain flour
4 oz (110 g) mixed peel

2 level tsp mixed spice
4 oz (110 g) walnuts, finely chopped
8 oz (225 g) sultanas
8 oz (225 g) seedless raisins
8-12 tbsp Guinness

Preheat the oven to 325°F/170°C/Gas Mk 3. Grease and line an 8 inch (20 cm) round cake tin. Cream the butter and sugar together until light and fluffy in colour and texture. Gradually beat in the eggs, a little at a time. If the mixture curdles add a little sifted flour. Sift the flour and mixed spice together and fold into the creamed mixture with a metal spoon. Gently stir in the raisins, sultanas, mixed peel and chopped walnuts. Stir 4 tablespoons of Guinness into the mixture to form a soft dropping consistency. Spoon into the cake tin and bake in the centre of the oven for 1 hour, then reduce the heat to 300°F/150°C/Gas Mk 2 and cook for another 1½ hours. Leave in the tin for about 30 minutes before turning out to cool on a wire tray. Prick the base of the cake with a skewer and spoon over the remaining Guinness. Keep the cake in a tin for one week before eating.

APPLE CRUMBLE CAKE
Makes 8-10 slices

4 oz (110 g) soft margarine
4 oz (110 g) caster sugar
½ tsp vanilla essence
2 eggs, beaten
6 oz (150 g) self-raising flour, sifted

pinch of salt
1 tbsp milk, optional
12 oz (350 g) cooking apples,
    peeled, cored and sliced

Topping: 3 oz (75 g) hard margarine
      4 oz (110 g) self-raising flour, sifted
      3 oz (75 g) caster sugar
      1 tbsp water

Line and grease a deep round 8 inch (20 cm) loose-bottomed cake tin. Preheat the oven to 350°F/180°C/Gas Mk 3. Cream fat with sugar till pale and fluffy. Beat in vanilla essence and then the eggs, one at a time. Gently fold in flour and salt using a metal spoon. Moisten with milk, if necessary, to make a fairly stiff dropping consistency. Turn into cake tin. Arrange sliced apples over top. To make the topping rub margarine into flour, stir in sugar and water. Sprinkle the topping over. Bake in centre of the oven for 1¼ hours or until light and golden. Cool in the tin.

SPICY DATE CAKE
Makes an 8 inch (20 cm) round cake

8 oz (225 g) butter
8 oz (225 g) caster sugar
3 large eggs, beaten
8 oz (225 g) chopped dates

2 level tsp mixed spice
10 oz (275 g) plain flour, sifted
1 level tsp baking powder
pinch of salt

Preheat the oven to 350°F/180°C/ Gas Mk 4, then grease and line an 8 inch (20 cm) round cake tin. Sift the flour, salt, baking powder and mixed spice together. Cream the butter and sugar together until light and fluffy in colour and texture. Beat in the eggs, a little at a time, adding a little flour if the mixture curdles. Stir 2 tbsp flour mix into the chopped dates. Fold the flour and dates alternately into the creamed mixture using a metal spoon. Spoon into the prepared cake tin and bake on the centre shelf of the oven then turn the gas down 325°F/160°C/Gas Mk 3 and cook for another 1½ hours or until a warm skewer pushed into the cake comes out clean. Leave the cake to cool in the tin for 30 minutes, then turn onto a wire tray, removing the lining paper.

DUNDEE CAKE
Makes a 7 inch (18 cm) round cake

2 oz (50 g) shelled almonds, skinned
6 oz (175 g) butter
6 oz (175 g) soft brown sugar
3 eggs
1 level tsp baking powder
1½ oz (40 g) ground almonds

5 oz (150 g) sultanas
5 oz (150 g) currants
1½ oz (40 g) cut mixed peel
6 oz (175 g) plain flour
1 tbsp milk

Preheat the oven to 300°F/150°C/Gas Mk 2. Brush a deep round 7 inch (18 cm) cake tin with melted fat and line base and side with a double thickness of oiled or greased greaseproof paper Cream butter and sugar together until light and fluffy. Beat eggs together and add gradually, beating well after each addition. Mix in ground almonds, sultanas, currants and mixed peel. Sift flour and baking powder together and fold into mixture, alternatiing with the milk, cutting through mixture with a metal spoon. Place mixture in cake tin and level top with back of spoon. Arrange almonds in rings on top of cake and gently press into cake mixture. Bake just below centre of oven for 3¼ to 3½ hours. Test by pressing with the fingers. If cooked, the cake should spring back, have stopped bubbling and have begun to shrink from side of tin. Remove from oven and leave to cool in tin for 30 minutes. Turn out, remove paper and cool on a wire rack.

HALF POUND CAKE
Makes an 8 inch (20 cm) cake

8 oz (225 g) butter
8 oz (225 g) caster sugar
4 eggs, beaten
8 oz (225 g) plain white flour, sifted
pinch of salt
1 tbsp brandy

8 oz (225 g) seedless raisins
8 oz (225 g) mixed currants & sultanas
4 oz (110 g) glacé cherries,
 washed and chopped
½ tsp ground mixed spice

Topping: walnut halves

Preheat the oven to 300°F/150°C/Gas Mk 2. Grease a deep 8 inch (20 cm) round cake tin and line with greaseproof paper. In a bowl, cream together the butter and sugar until fluffy. Gradually beat in the eggs. Fold in the flour, fruit, salt and spice and add enough brandy to bring the mixture to a soft dropping consistency. Pile the cake mixture into the tin, level the top and decorate with walnut halves. Bake for approximately 2½ hours. Leave in cake tin for 30 minutes before transferring to a wire rack to cool.

CHERRY CAKE
Makes a 10 inch (25 cm) round cake

8 oz (225 g) butter or soft
margarine, softened
8 oz (225 g) caster sugar
4 eggs, beaten
6 oz (175 g) glacé cherries,
washed, dried and chopped

12 oz (350 g) plain flour, sifted
pinch of salt
2 tsp baking powder
few drops vanilla essence
milk to mix

Preheat the oven to 350°F/180°C/Gas Mk 4. Grease and line a 10 in
(25 cm) cake tin. Cream the butter or margarine with the caster sugar
until very soft and fluffy. Gradually beat the eggs into the mixture a
little at a time (a spoonful of the sieved flour can be added if the mixture curdles). Roll the chopped cherries in flour and add to the mixture with the vanilla essence. Sift the remaining flour, salt and baking
powder together and fold gently into the creamed mixture with a
metal spoon. Stir, adding milk if necessary, to obtain a fairly stiff
dropping consistency. Bake for 1-1¼ hours.

UPSIDE-DOWN PLUM CAKE
Makes 12-16 slices

Fruit base:
4 tbsp plum or raspberry jam
1 lb (450 g) Victoria plums, stoned and cut into quarters

Sponge topping:
3 eggs
3 oz (75 g) caster sugar
2½ oz (65 g) plain flour

¼ tsp ground cinnamon
1½ oz (40 g) butter, melted

Preheat the oven to 350°F/180°C/Gas Mk 4. Grease a Swiss roll tin.
Melt the jam with 1 tablespoon water in a small pan then pour evenly
over the base of the tin. Arrange the plum quarters in rows on top. To
make the sponge, whisk the eggs with the sugar until pale and very
thick. The mixture should leave a trail when the whisk is lifted.
Gradually fold in the flour and cinnamon, then, when completely
incorporated, fold in the melted butter. Pour the mixture over the top
of the plums, then bake for 25-30 minutes or until the sponge is gold-
en and springs back when lightly pressed. To serve the cake, carefully
run a knife round the edges of the cake, place a cooling rack over the
top of the tin, then turn over. Remove from the tin and allow the cake
to cool. Cut into slices before serving.

BANANA YOGHURT CAKE
Makes a 9 inch (23 cm) deep square cake

8 oz (225 g) flour
¾ tsp salt
3 tsp baking powder
¼ tsp bicarbonate of soda
6 oz (175 g) butter
6 oz (175 g) caster sugar
2 eggs

1 tsp grated lemon rind
1 tsp vanilla essence
4 bananas
2 tbsp lemon juice
4 oz (110 g) yoghurt
4 small bananas for decoration

Icing: 3 oz (75 g) butter
12 oz (350 g) sifted icing sugar
3 tbsp milk
1 tsp vanilla essence

Preheat the oven to 350°F/180°C/Gas Mk 4. Grease and base-line a 9 inch (23 cm) deep square cake tin. Sift the flour, salt, baking powder and bicarbonate of soda together twice. Cream the butter and sugar together until light and fluffy. Add the eggs, one at a time, beating well after each addition. Stir in the lemon rind and vanilla essence. Peel the bananas and mash. Squeeze a little lemon juice over the bananas and mix together, then stir in the yoghurt. Sift the dry ingredients into the creamed butter and sugar, alternately with the bananas. Beat well for 1 minute using a wooden spoon. Pour into the prepared cake tin and bake on the middle shelf of the oven for 40-45 minutes. Remove from the oven and cool in the tin for 10 minutes before turning out onto a wire rack. For the icing, cream the butter and beat in half the sifted icing sugar. Add the milk and vanilla essence and beat in the remaining icing sugar to make a soft icing. When the cake is cold spread the icing on the top and round the sides of the cake. Slice the bananas and dip in lemon juice to keep them from discolouring. Arrange in rows on top of the icing.

CHERRY AND DATE CAKE

8 oz (225 g) margarine
6 oz (175 g) caster sugar
3 large eggs, beaten
½ tsp vanilla essence
12 oz (350 g) plain flour
2 tsp baking powder

½ tsp mixed spice
pinch of salt
6 oz (175 g) glacé cherries, rinsed,
    thoroughly dried and halved
6 oz (175 g) chopped dates
5 fl oz (150 ml) cold tea

Preheat the oven to 325°F/170°C/Gas Mk 3. Grease a 7 inch (18 cm) square cake tin and line with greased greaseproof paper. Place the margarine and sugar in a bowl and cream until light and fluffy. Gradually add the eggs, beating well, then the vanilla essence. In another bowl, mix together the flour, baking powder, mixed spice and salt. Gradually fold the flour mixture and the peel, cherries and dates into the margarine and sugar mixture and then gradually pour in the tea. The mixture should be fairly moist. Transfer to the prepared cake tin, levelling the top and making a slight hollow in the centre of the cake. Bake in the oven for about 2 hours until a knife inserted in the middle of the cake comes out clean. Leave to cool in the tin.

PUMPKIN CAKE
Makes a 7 inch (18 cm) square cake

4 oz (110 g) self-raising flour
1 tsp ground cinnamon
¼ tsp freshly grated nutmeg
½ tsp salt
1 medium egg
1½ oz (40 g) soft margarine
  plus extra for greasing

2 oz (50 g) caster sugar
2 oz (50 g) soft light brown sugar
8 fl oz (225 ml) pumpkin purée,
  fresh or canned
2 oz (50 g) raisins

Frosting: ½ oz (15 g) soft margarine
  grated zest of 1 lemon
  4 oz (110 g) icing sugar, sifted
  1 tsp lemon juice
  1 tbsp thick cream

Preheat the oven to 350°F/180°C/Gas Mk 4. Grease a 7 inch (18 cm) square cake tin. Sift together the flour, cinnamon, nutmeg and salt and beat in the egg. In another bowl, cream together the margarine and sugars and beat until light. Beat the dry ingredients and pumpkin purée alternately into the margarine mixture, then stir in the nuts and raisins. Turn the mixture into the tin and bake in centre of oven for 45-50 minutes until the cake is done. Leave to cool in the tin, then turn out. Make the frosting, cream together the margarine and lemon zest, add the sugar, lemon juice and cream, and beat until smooth. Spread the frosting on top of the cold cake. Draw a fork from side to side, making parallel lines in one direction. Then draw it across 3 or 4 times in the opposite direction to make a wavy pattern. Cut the pumpkin cake into 8 fingers and serve.

ORANGE HONEY CAKE
Makes a 7 inch (18 cm) deep round cake

4 oz (110 g) butter or soft margarine
6 oz (175 g) caster sugar
2 eggs, beaten
5 fl oz (150 ml) carton natural yoghurt

6 fl oz (175 ml) concentrated orange
  juice
6 oz (175 g) self-raising flour, sifted

Orange honey cream:
2 oz (50 g) butter or soft margarine
6 fl oz (175 ml) concentrated orange juice

2 level tbsp honey
6 oz (175 g) icing sugar

Preheat the oven to 357°F/190°C/Gas Mk 5. Grease and line the bottom of two 7 in (18 cm) sandwich tins. Cream the butter or margarine and the sugar together until fluffy and pale in colour. Beat in the eggs one at a time. Mix the orange juice and yoghurt together and stir into the mixture. Fold in the flour gently with a metal spoon and pour into the tins. Bake in the centre of the oven for about 25 minutes or until golden brown and firm to the touch. Turn out and leave to cool on a wire rack. To make the orange honey cream, gently melt the butter or margarine with the honey in a small saucepan and leave to cool. Stir in the orange juice and icing sugar. Beat for 1 minute until well blended and use to sandwich the cakes together and ice the top.

QUICK CHERRY ALMOND CAKE
Makes a 10 inch (25 cm) cake

8 oz (225 g) soft margarine
8 oz (225 g) caster sugar
4 eggs, lightly beaten
12 oz (350 g) plain flour, sifted
1 oz (25 g) flaked almonds
pinch of salt

10 oz (250 g) sultanas
6 oz (150 g) glacé cherries, washed,
  dried and chopped
1 oz (25 g) ground almonds
few drops vanilla essence
1 tsp baking powder

Preheat the oven to 300°F/150°C/Gas Mk 2. Grease and line a 10 inch (25 cm) cake tin. Cream the softened butter or margarine with the caster sugar until very soft and fluffy.Beat the eggs together lightly and gradually beat into the mixture a little at a time - a little of the flour can be added if the mixture curdles. Roll the chopped cherries and sultanas in flour and add to the mixture with the vanilla essence. Sift the flour, salt and baking powder together, add the ground almonds and fold gently into the creamed mixture with a metal spoon. Stir, adding milk if necessary, to obtain a smooth, stiff dropping consistency. Spoon the mixture into the prepared cake tin, sprinkle over the flaked almonds and bake for 1-1¼ hours.

GREEK YOGHURT CAKE
Makes an 8 inch (20 cm) round cake

2 oz (50 g) butter
3 eggs, separated
½ oz (15 g) caster sugar
1 carton natural yoghurt

grated rind of 1 lemon
6 oz (175 g) plain flour
2 level tsp bicarbonate of soda
½ level tsp salt

Icing:
2 oz (50 g) icing sugar, sifted
2 tbsp lemon juice

grated rind of 1 lemon
fresh lemon slices for decoration

Preheat the oven to 350°F/180°C/Gas Mk 4. Grease and flour an 8 inch (20 cm) round cake tin. Cream the butter and sugar together until light and fluffy, then add the beaten egg yolks, mixing well. Add the yoghurt and the lemon rind. Beat well, then gradually sift in the flour with the bicarbonate of soda and salt. Whisk the egg whites until just stiff and fold into the cake mixture. Pour into the prepared cake tin and bake for 1¼ hours, or until an inserted skewer comes out clean. Turn out and leave to cool on a wire rack. Mix the icing sugar with the lemon rind and juice. Pour over the top of the cake and leave to set. Decorate with slices of fresh lemon just before serving. The cake tastes better after storing for two days.

PEAR AND NUT CAKE
Makes a 7 inch (18 cm) cake

1¼ lb (560 g) pears,
  peeled and cored
3 oz (75 g) butter
3 tbsp clear honey
2 eggs, beaten

4 oz (110 g) self-raising wholemeal
  flour, sifted
1 tsp baking powder
½ tsp ground mace
2 oz (50 g) walnuts, shelled and chopped

Preheat the oven to 375°F/190°C/Gas Mk 5. Place three-quarters of the pears in a blender and purée until smooth. In a bowl, cream the butter and honey together and gradually add the eggs. Add the flour, baking powder, mace and walnuts and mix well, then stir in the pear purée. Thinly slice the remaining pears. Place half the cake mixture in a greased 7 inch (18 cm) deep round cake tin lined with greaseproof paper. Arrange the pear slices on top and then cover with the remaining cake mixture. Bake in oven for 1 hour, or until a warmed skewer inserted in the centre of cake comes out clean. Cool in tin before turning out onto a wire rack. Leave for 24 hours before serving.

CARROT AND DATE CAKE
Makes a 2 lb (1 kg) cake

6 oz (175 g) butter, softened
6 oz (175 g) light soft brown sugar
3 eggs, separated
grated zest and juice of ½ orange
4 oz (110 g) self-raising flour, sifted
½ tsp baking powder

pinch grated nutmeg
2 oz (50 g) ground almonds
8 oz (225 g) carrots,
    peeled and finely grated
6 oz (175 g) stoned dates, chopped
3 tbsp clear honey

Topping:
8 oz (225 g) low-fat cream cheese   2 tbsp caster sugar

Preheat the oven to 350°F/180°C/Gas Mk 4. Grease and line a 2 lb (1 kg) loaf tin. Cream the butter and sugar until pale and fluffy. Beat in the egg yolks, then stir in orange zest and 1 tbsp orange juice. Sift in flour, baking powder and nutmeg, then stir in almonds. Whisk egg whites until stiff and fold in with carrots. Mix the dates with 2 tbsp honey. Spoon half the cake mixture into the tin, cover with the dates and honey, then top with the remaining mixture. Bake for 1¼-1½ hours. Cool slightly in the tin, then turn out on to wire rack. Beat the cream cheese, sugar, remaining honey and 1 tbsp orange juice together and spread on top.

OLD-FASHIONED SULTANA CAKE
Makes a 7 inch (18 cm) deep round cake

10 oz (300 g) self-raising flour, sifted
5 oz (150 g) butter or soft margarine
5 oz (150 g) caster sugar
6 oz (175 g) sultanas
2 oz (50 g) mixed peel

1 small lemon
good pinch freshly grated nutmeg
2 eggs
5-6 tbsp milk
demerara sugar for sprinkling on top

Preheat the oven to 375°F/190°C/Gas Mk 5. Grease and line a deep 7 inch (18 cm) round cake tin. Sift the flour into a mixing bowl and rub in the butter or margarine until the mixture resembles fine breadcrumbs. Stir in the sugar, sultanas and mixed peel. Grate the lemon rind and add to the mixture with the grated nutmeg. Beat the eggs and milk together lightly and mix into the flour mixture. Stir until a soft dropping consistency is achieved, adding more milk if necessary. Turn into the tin and bake on the lower centre shelf for 1-1¼ hours until the cake is golden brown and springy to the touch. Turn out onto a wire rack to cool and remove the greaseproof paper Sprinkle with demerara sugar and cool.

JOHN PEEL CAKE
Makes an 8 inch (20 cm) round cake

12 oz (350 g) plain flour, sifted
12 oz (350 g) currants, cleaned
4 level tsp ground cinnamon
chopped peel
½ level tsp mixed spice
6 oz (175 g) soft light brown sugar
1 level tsp bicarbonate of soda

good pinch of salt
6 oz (175 g) mixed peel
¼ level tsp ground nutmeg
grated rind of 1 orange
2½ oz (65g) margarine
½ pt (300 ml) milk

Preheat the oven to 350°F/180°C/Gas Mk 4. Grease and line an 8 inch (20 cm) round cake tin. Sift the flour, salt, cinnamon, nutmeg and mixed spice together into a mixing bowl. Add the margarine cut into small pieces and rub in until the mixture resembles fine breadcrumbs. Stir in the sugar, currants, peel and orange rind. Warm 2 tbsp of the milk and dissolve the bicarbonate of soda in it. Mix the rest of the milk into the dry ingredients, then stir in the bicarbonate mixture and mix well. Turn into the tin and bake on the centre shelf of the oven for 1 hour. Then reduce the heat to 325°F/160°C/Gas Mk 3 and cook for a further 1 hour. Test the cake by inserting a warm skewer into the cake. If it comes out clean the cake is cooked. Cool in the tin for 20 minutes, then turn out onto a wire tray, remove the lining paper and leave to cool.

YORKSHIRE PARKIN
Makes 30

1 level tsp bicarbonate of soda
12 oz (350 g) quick-cooking oatmeal
4 oz (110 g) plain flour, sifted
1 level tsp ground cinnamon
1 level tsp ground ginger
1 level tsp ground nutmeg

4 fl oz (125 ml) molasses
4 fl oz (125 ml) golden syrup
4 oz (110 g) soft butter
finely grated rind of 1 lemon
milk to mix

Preheat the oven to 350°F/180°C/Gas Mk 4. Blend together the soda, oatmeal, flour and spices. Beat together the molasses, golden syrup, butter, lemon rind and milk. Fold in the dry mixture and blend thoroughly. Pour into a greased Swiss roll tin and bake for 1¼ hours until browned. Cool on a wire rack and cut whilst still warm.

PEACH AND HAZELNUT DELIGHT
Makes an 8 inch (20 cm) cake

3 oz (75 g) plain flour
1 tsp powdered instant coffee
4 ¹/₂ oz (125 g) caster sugar
¹/₄ pt (150 ml) double cream
3 or 4 fresh peaches,
* peeled and sliced*

pinch of salt
3 eggs
2 oz (50 g) ground, toasted hazelnuts
clear honey

Preheat the oven to350°F/180°C/Gas Mk 4. Sift the flour, salt and powdered coffee together. Grease an 8 inch (20 cm) cake tin and line the bottom with greaseproof paper. Whisk the eggs with the sugar in a bowl set over a saucepan of gently simmering hot water until they are thick and foamy. Remove from the saucepan and keep whisking until the mixture is cool, then fold in the flour and the nuts very gently with a metal spoon. Pour into the tin and bake for 30-35 minutes, testing after 25 minutes. Cool on a wire tray. When the cake is cold slice across into two. Whip the cream with a little honey until firm and mix with the peach slices. Pile on the bottom layer of the cake and top with the second layer. A little cream and peaches can be spread over the top with chopped hazelnuts if desired.

CARAMEL GLORY CAKE
Serves 8-10

8 oz (225 g) mixed dried fruit
4 oz (125 g) glacé cherries, chopped
2 oz (50 g) crystallised peel, chopped
4 oz (125 g) mixed nuts, chopped
8 oz (225 g) digestive biscuits
6 oz (175 g) unsalted butter
6 tbsp golden syrup
double cream (optional)

Mix the fruit, peel and nuts together in a large bowl. Roughly crush half the biscuits into small pieces and finely crumble the remaining half. Mix in with the fruit and nuts. Put the butter and syrup in a saucepan and heat gently until the butter has melted, then boil for 2-3 minutes. Leave to cool for a few minutes, then pour over the fruit and nut mixture, and mix thoroughly. Spoon the mixture into a buttered 8 inch (20 cm) loose-bottomed cake tin and put in the refrigerator to set overnight. When ready to serve, turn out onto a plate and cover with whipped cream if desired.

APPLE CIDER CAKE
Makes a deep 8 inch (20 cm) cake

6 oz (175 g) soft margarine
6 oz (175 g) caster sugar
3 eggs

6 oz (175 g) self-raising flour
1½ level tsp baking powder
2 tbsp sweet cider

Filling:
2 cooking apples, peeled and sliced
1 rounded tsp grated lemon rind

2 oz (50 g) caster sugar
5 fl oz (150 ml) whipped cream

Topping:
8 oz (225 g) icing sugar, sifted

2 tbsp sweet cider

Preheat the oven to 350°F/180°C/Gas Mk 4. Beat all cake ingredients together until soft and creamy. Divide evenly between two 8 inch (20 cm) sandwich tins and bake in the centre of the oven for 25 minutes or until risen and golden. Turn out and cool on a wire rack. Put the apples in a pan with the sugar and lemon rind. Cover and simmer gently until soft. Beat to a purée and cool. When cold fold the purée into the whipped cream and sandwich the two cakes together. Sift 8 oz (225 g) icing sugar, mix to a smooth glacé icing with 2 tbsp sweet cider and spread over the cake.

SESAME SEED CAKE
Makes an 8 inch (20 cm) round cake

8 oz (225 g) margarine
13 oz (375 g) caster sugar
5 eggs, beaten
8 oz (225 g) plain flour
few drops vanilla essence
pinch of salt
3 tbsp sesame seeds

Preheat the oven to 325°F/170°C/Gas Mark 3. Lightly grease and flour an 8 inch (20 cm) round cake tin. Place the margarine and butter in a bowl and cream until fluffy. Gradually beat in the eggs, adding 2 tbsp of the flour with the last egg. Add vanilla essence to taste. Mix in the rest of the flour and salt and 2 tbsp of the sesame seeds. Mix thoroughly until well blended. Transfer the mixture to the prepared cake tin and level the surface. Sprinkle the remaining sesame seeds on top. Bake in the oven for 1½-2 hours until a knife inserted in the middle comes out clean. Turn out onto a wire tray to cool.

MUM'S FAVOURITE
Makes a 9 x 12 inch (23 x 30 cm) slab cake

4 oz (110 g) chopped dates
1 tsp bicarbonate of soda
6 oz (175 g) caster sugar
2 oz (50 g) butter
6 oz (175 g) plain flour, sifted

1 tsp baking powder
½ tsp salt
2 oz (50 g) walnuts, chopped
1 tsp vanilla essence
1 beaten egg

Topping:5 tbsp soft light brown sugar
*   2 tbsp butter*
*   2 tbsp cream from the top of the milk (or single cream)*
*   few whole walnuts*

Pour a cup of boiling water over the chopped dates and bicarbonate
of soda in a small bowl and allow to stand while mixing the cake.
Preheat the oven to 350°F/180°C/Gas Mk 4. Cream the butter and
sugar together, add the beaten egg and vanilla essence and finally sift
in the flour, salt and baking powder. Mix well then add the walnuts.
Drain the date mixture and add to the cake mixture. Line a 9 x 12 inch
(23 x 30 cm) Swiss roll tin with foil, building it up well at the sides.
Pour in the cake mix and bake for 30 minutes until firm to the touch.
Remove from the oven and leave to cool slightly. Put all the topping
ingredients in a medium-sized saucepan and bring to the boil. Simmer
gently without stirring for 3 minutes and then pour over the top of
the cake. Decorate with whole walnuts.

WALNUT CAKE
Makes a 7 inch (18 cm) deep cake

5 oz (150 g) butter
6 oz (175 g) caster sugar
2 eggs, beaten
½ tsp vanilla essence

8 oz (225 g) self-raising flour, sifted
3 oz (75 g) walnuts, roughly chopped
3 tbsp milk

Icing: 1 lb (450 g) lump sugar
*   ¼pt (150 ml) water*
*   large pinch cream of tartar*
*   2 egg whites, stiffly beaten*
*   1 tsp vanilla essence*
*   9 walnut halves*

Preheat the oven to 350°F/180°C/Gas Mk 4. Grease and line a 7 inch
(18 cm) deep cake tin. Cream the softened butter and caster sugar
together, then beat in the eggs and vanilla essence. Fold in the sifted

flour with a metal spoon, stirring in the chopped walnuts gradually and adding the milk to obtain a soft but firm dropping consistency. Spoon into the tin and bake for 1¼ hours. Leave to cool on a wire rack. To make the icing, dissolve the sugar in the water over a gentle heat. When dissolved turn the heat up and add the cream of tartar. Bring to the boil and boil gently without stirring to a soft ball stage. Test by dropping a tiny bit into cold water. If it forms a soft ball, it is ready. Pour immediately onto the stiffly beaten egg whites, stirring until the mixture is very thick and almost setting. Flavour with the vanilla essence and pour over the cooled cake, smoothing with a knife dipped in boiling water. Decorate with the walnut halves.

LIGHT FRUIT CAKE
Makes a 6 inch (15 cm) deep round cake

6 oz (175 g) self-raising flour, sifted
pinch of salt
4 oz (110 g) butter or softened
    margarine
4 oz (110 g) caster sugar
grated rind of ½ orange
2 eggs, beaten

2 oz (50 g) glacé cherries, rinsed,
    dried and chopped
1 oz (25 g) angelica, chopped
1½ oz (40 g) crystallised ginger, chopped
1½ oz (40 g) walnuts, chopped
1 tbsp hot water
1 oz (25 g) sultanas

Topping: 2 level tbsp apricot jam
    1 tbsp water
    1-2 oz (25-50 g) glacé cherries
    4 shelled walnut halves

Preheat the oven to 350°F/180°C/Gas Mk 4. Grease and line a 6 inch (15 cm) round cake tin. Sift the flour with the salt. Cream the butter or margarine with the sugar until light and fluffy, add the orange rind and beat. Pour in the egg, a little at a time, beating well between each addition, then fold in the flour very gently with a metal spoon. Pour the orange juice into the hot water, add to the cake mixture with the chopped fruit and nuts and fold in until evenly mixed. Spoon into the tin and bake in the centre of the oven for 1-1¼ hours until golden brown. Test with a skewer until it comes out clean. Turn out onto a wire rack, remove the lining paper and leave to cool. To make the topping, heat the apricot jam with the water in a small saucepan, sieve to make smooth, and spread over the top of the cake. Cut the glacé cherries in half. Cut the walnut halves in half again. Arrange around the top edge of the cake.

LEMON AND ALMOND CAKE
Makes an 8 inch (20 cm) round cake

6 oz (175 g) margarine
6 oz (175 g) caster sugar
3 eggs, beaten
2 oz (50 g) lemon curd
finely grated rind of ½ large lemon

few drops almond essence
2 oz (50 g) ground almonds
6 oz (175 g) self-raising flour
1 oz (25 g) flaked almonds

Preheat the oven to 325°F/170°C/Gas Mk 3. Grease and line an 8 inch (20 cm) round cake tin. Put the margarine and sugar in a bowl and cream until soft. Gradually beat in the eggs, followed by the lemon curd and lemon rind, and add almond essence to taste. Fold in the flour and ground almonds and mix until thoroughly blended. Transfer to the cake tin, level the top and sprinkle over the flaked almonds. Bake for 1-1½ hours until a knife inserted in the middle of the cake comes out clean. Leave to cool in the tin for 5 minutes before turning out onto a wire rack and removing the greaseproof paper.

POLISH WALNUT CAKE
Makes a 7 inch (18 cm) deep cake

4 oz (110 g) chopped walnuts
grated rind of 2 oranges
1 oz (25 g) breadcrumbs

4 eggs, separated
8 oz (225 g) caster sugar

Filling:
3 oz (75 g) chopped walnuts
2 oz (50 g) icing sugar
4 tbsp soured cream

⅛ tsp vanilla essence
3 oz (75 g) icing sugar
a few walnut halves for decoration

Preheat the oven to 350°F/180°C/Gas Mk 4. Grease and base line two 7 inch (18 cm) sandwich tins. Mix the walnuts with the grated orange rind and breadcrumbs. Put the egg yolks and sugar in a bowl over a pan of hot water and whisk until thick and pale. Whisk the egg whites until stiff and then fold into the egg mixture together with the nut mixture. Divide the mixture between the tins. Bake in the centre of the oven for about 45 minutes. Leave to cool in the tins for 10 minutes, then turn out. Cover with a clean tea towel and leave overnight. To make the filling, mix the nuts with the icing sugar, soured cream and vanilla essence, and use to sandwich the cakes together. Mix the icing sugar with enough water to make a coating consistency, spread over the top of the cake and decorate with walnut halves.

LARDY CAKE

8 oz (225 g) strong plain flour
¼ tsp salt
¼ tsp mixed spice
¼ oz (5 g) fresh yeast

¼ pint (150 ml) warm milk
2 oz (50 g) lard
2 oz (50 g) + 1 tsp sugar
2 oz (50 g) mixed dried fruit

Preheat the oven to 450°F/230°C/Gas Mk 8. Put the flour, salt and mixed spice in a warm bowl. Cream the yeast with 1 tsp sugar and add to the flour with the warm milk to make a soft dough. Beat thoroughly, cover and leave in a warm place for about 45 minutes until the dough has doubled in size. On a floured board, roll out the dough to form an oblong, ¼ inch (0.5 cm) thick. Spread over half the lard, half the remaining sugar and half the dried fruit. Fold in three, then roll out again into an oblong shape. Spread over the remaining lard, sugar and dried fruit. Roll out to an oblong 1 inch (2.5 cm) thick to fit into a deep cake tin. Leave the mixture in the cake tin in a warm place for 1 hour until it is well risen. Score the top with a knife, brush with a little sugar dissolved in water and bake in the oven for 30 minutes.

SPONGE CAKES

ALMOND CAKE
Makes a 6 inch (15 cm) cake

4 oz (110 g) plain flour, sifted
1 level tsp baking powder
4 oz (110 g) butter
6 oz (175 g) caster sugar

2 eggs, beaten
2 oz (50 g) ground almonds
2 drops almond essence
2 tbsp milk

Preheat the oven to 325°F/160°C/Gas Mk 3. Grease and line a 6 inch (15 cm) round cake tin. Sift the flour and baking powder together. Cream the butter and sugar together until light and fluffy then beat in the eggs, adding a little flour if the mixture curdles. Fold in the ground almonds, almond essence and flour alternately using a metal spoon, adding enough milk to make a soft but firm mixture. Spoon into the prepared cake tin and bake on the centre shelf of the oven for 1½ hours or until the cake is cooked. Test by pushing a warm skewer into cake. Leave the cake to cool in the tin for 30 minutes, then turn onto a wire tray, removing the lining paper and allow to cool completely.

BUTTERSCOTCH CAKE
Makes 8 slices

6 oz (175 g) butter or soft margarine
6 oz (175 g) caster sugar
3 eggs, beaten
6 oz (175 g) self-raising flour, sifted
2-3 tbsp water

Icing:
1 egg, separated
2 oz (50 g) icing sugar
4 oz (110 g) butter or soft margarine
½ tsp butterscotch essence
3 oz (75 g) peanut brittle

Preheat the oven to 350°F/180°C/Gas Mk 4. Cream the butter or margarine together with the sugar until light and fluffy. Add the beaten eggs a little at a time, beating well after each addition. Sprinkle half the flour and 1 tbsp water over the creamed mixture and fold it in with a metal spoon. Fold in the rest of the flour and another tbsp water, adding more water if necessary. Grease and base line a large Swiss roll tin and spread the mixture over the tin. Bake on the centre shelf of the oven for 20-25 minutes until firm and springy to the touch. Turn onto a wire tray and leave to cool. Trim the edges when cold and cut into three 3 inch (7.5 cm) wide strips. To make the the the icing, whisk the egg white until it starts to stiffen, then add the sifted icing sugar. Stand the bowl over a pan of boiling water, whisking for 3-4 minutes until the icing is stiff and glossy. Remove from the heat. Cream the butter or margarine until soft, then beat in the egg yolk and essence. Gradually mix into the icing to give a soft texture. Cover the bowl and chill in the fridge for 30 minutes. Put 2 oz (50 g) peanut brittle into a plastic bag and crush with a rolling pin. Break the remainder into evenly sized pieces. Spread half the icing over two of the cake strips and sprinkle with crushed peanut brittle. Place one on top of the other. Place the third slice on top and spread with the rest of the icing. Swirl the icing with a fork and decorate the edges with the peanut brittle pieces.

VICTORIA SPONGE 1

Makes two 8 inch (20 cm) sandwich cakes

6 oz *(175 g) butter or soft margarine*
6 oz *(175 g) caster sugar*
3 eggs, beaten

6 oz *(175 g) self-raising flour, sifted*
2-3 tbsp water

Filling and topping
3-4 level tbsp apricot jam
1-2 tbsp sifted icing sugar
whipped cream (optional)

Preheat the oven to 350°F/180°C/Gas Mk 4. Grease and line the base of two 8 inch (20 cm) sandwich tins. Cream the butter or margarine together with the sugar until light and fluffy. Add the beaten eggs a little at a time, beating well after each addition. Sprinkle half the flour and 1 tablespoon of water over the creamed mixture and fold it in with a metal spoon. Fold in the rest of the flour and another tablespoon water. Mix well, spread the cake mixture into the tins and level the tops. Bake in the centre of the oven for 25 minutes or until the cakes are golden brown and firm to the touch. Leave the cakes to cool in the tins for 2-3 minutes before turning out onto a wire rack to cool. When cold remove the lining paper. Sandwich the cakes together with a generous layer of jam, plus whipped cream if liked, and dust the top with icing sugar.

VICTORIA SPONGE 2

Makes two 7 inch (18 cm) round sandwich cakes

4 oz *(110 g) butter or soft margarine*
4 oz *(110 g) caster sugar*
2 eggs, beaten

4 oz *(110 g) self-raising flour, sifted*
3-4 level tbsp red jam
1-2 tbsp icing sugar

Preheat the oven to 350°F/180°C/Gas Mk 4. Grease and flour two 7 inch (18 cm) sandwich tins. Cream the butter or margarine together with the sugar until light and fluffy in colour and texture. Add the beaten eggs a little at a time, beating well after each addition. Add a little sifted flour in between the eggs to avoid curdling. Fold in the rest of the flour gently with a metal spoon. Spread the cake mixture into the tins and level the tops. Bake in the centre of the oven for 25 minutes or until the cakes are golden brown and firm to the touch. Leave the cakes to cool in the tins for 2-3 minutes before turning out onto a wire rack to cool. Sandwich the cakes together with a layer of jam, plus whipped cream if liked, and dust the top with icing sugar.

CHOCOLATE CAKE
Makes two 7 inch (18 cm) sandwich cakes or one 8 inch (20 cm) cake

Use recipe for Victoria sponge 2 on page 25,
substituting1 level tbsp cocoa powder for 1 tbsp of the flour

Make the cake as directed on page 25 . Fill with cocoa-flavoured butter cream icing and top with chocolate fudge icing.

COFFEE AND WALNUT CAKE
Makes two 7 inch (18 cm) round cakes

Use recipe for Victoria sponge 2 on page 25, adding 1 level tbsp instant
coffee powder dissolved in 2 tbsp hot water

Make the cake as directed on page 25 and fill with butter cream icing (plain or coffee flavoured as preferred) mixed with chopped walnuts. Top with coffee glacé icing and arrange walnut halves on top.

GINGER SPONGE CAKE
Makes two 7 inch (18 cm) cakes

Use recipe for Victoria sponge 2 on page 25, adding 1 level tsp ground ginger
and 1 level tbsp ginger syrup from preserved ginger

Make the cake as directed on page 25 and fill with plain butter cream icing with 1 tablespoon chopped preserved ginger added. Top with white glacé icing and arrange pieces of preserved ginger around the edge.

CHOCOLATE CUP CAKES
Makes 12

Use recipe for Victoria sponge 1 on page 25, substituting 1 level tbsp cocoa
powder for 1 level tbsp flour

Topping:
chocolate fudge icing

Preheat the oven to 375°F/190°C/Gas Mk 5. Make the cake mixture as directed on page 25 and half fill small cake cases. Bake in centre of the oven for 15 minutes.

LEMON CAKE
Makes an 8 inch (20 cm) sandwich cake

Use recipe for Victoria sponge 2 on page 25, adding the grated rind of a whole lemon to the cake mix

Make the cake as directed on page 25 and fill with 2 tbsp lemon curd mixed with 2 tbsp whipped double cream. Top with lemon glacé icing.

ORANGE CAKE
Makes an 8 inch (20 cm) sandwich cake

Use recipe for Victoria sponge 2 on page 25, adding grated rind of 1 orange and 1 tbsp concentrated orange juice to the cake mixture

Make the cake as directed on page 25 and fill with 2 tbsp orange marmalade. Top with orange glacé or butter cream icing.

BUTTERFLY CAKES
Makes 12

Use recipe for Victoria sponge 1 on page 25. using 6 oz (175 g) quantity

Preheat the oven to 375°F/190°C/Gas Mk 5. Make the cake as directed on page 25 and use the mixture to fill small cake cases. Bake in centre of the oven for 15 minutes. When cold, cut off the tops and cut these in half. Pipe a rosette of butter cream icing on top of each cake and replace the halved tops like wings. Dust with icing sugar.

CHERRY CAKES
Makes 12

Use recipe for Victoria sponge 1 on page 25, adding 2 oz (50 g) chopped glacé cherries

Preheat the oven to 375°F/190°C/Gas Mk 5. Make the cake mixture as directed on page 25 and use to fill small cake cases. Bake in the centre of the oven for 15 minutes.

CHOCOLATE MADELEINES
Makes 12

Use recipe for Victoria sponge 1 on page 25, substituting 1 level tbsp cocoa powder for 1 level tbsp flour

Topping:
6 tbsp sieved raspberry jam
6 heaped tbsp desiccated coconut
12 glacé cherries, halved

Preheat the oven to 375°F/190°C/Gas Mk 5. Make cake mixture as directed on page 25 and use to fill greased dariole moulds. Bake in centre of the oven for 15-20 minutes. When cold turn out and coat with warmed, sieved raspberry jam and roll in desiccated coconut. Top each with half a glacé cherry.

SPOTTED DICK CAKE
Makes a 10 inch (25 cm) round cake

8 oz (225 g) butter or soft margarine
8 oz (225 g) soft brown sugar
4 eggs, beaten
12 oz (350 g) plain flour, sifted

pinch of salt
2 tsp baking powder
6 oz (175 g) chocolate polka dots
milk to mix

Preheat the oven to 350°F/180°C/Gas Mk 4. Grease and line a 10 inch (25 cm) cake tin. Cream the softened butter or margarine with the brown sugar until very soft and fluffy. Gradually beat the eggs into the mixture, a little at a time (a little of the sieved flour can be added if the mixture curdles). Sift the flour again with the salt and baking powder. Fold gently into the creamed mixture with a metal spoon. Add the polka dots and milk, if necessary, mixing gently to a smooth, stiff dropping consistency. Turn into the tin and smooth the top. Bake for 1-1¼ hours. Allow to cool slightly before turning out.

BOOZY BAKE
Makes an 8 inch (20 cm) cake

4 oz (110 g) margarine or butter
8 oz (225 g) caster sugar
2 eggs ,beaten
1 oz (25 g) cocoa powder

1 x 9 fl oz (250 ml) can stout
8 oz (225 g) plain flour
1 level tsp bicarbonate of soda

Grease and base line an 8 inch (20 cm) spring clip tin. Preheat the oven to 350°F/180°C/Gas Mk 4. Cream together the butter or margarine with the sugar, then gradually add the eggs, beating well to mix. Blend the cocoa powder and a little stout to a smooth paste, then stir in the remainder of the stout. Sift the flour and bicarbonate of soda together, and mix them alternately with the stout liquid into the creamed mixture, beating well. Pour the mixture into the tin and cook for about 1¼ hours or until the cake is firm and springy.

APRICOT UPSIDE-DOWN CAKE
Makes an 8 inch (20 cm) cake

Use recipe for Victoria sponge 1 on page 25

Topping:
1 medium can apricot halves, drained
2-3 tbsp soft brown sugar
1 tbsp softened butter

Preheat the oven to 350°F/180°C/Gas Mk 4. Make the cake as directed on page 25. Coat an 8 inch (20 cm) loose-bottomed cake tin with softened butter and sprinkle 2 tbsp brown sugar on the base. Stand on a baking tray. Place the drained tinned apricot halves rounded sides down on the sugared base and cover with the sponge mixture. Bake in centre of the oven for 35-45 minutes. Turn out while hot and serve with cream or the remainder of the apricots, sieved or puréed and warmed as a sauce. Eat cold as a cake if preferred.

MARMALADE CAKE
Makes an 8 inch (20 cm) cake

4 oz (110 g) soft margarine
4 oz (110 g) caster sugar
2 eggs, beaten
4 oz (110 g) self-raising flour, sifted

5 tbsp chunky marmalade
1 tbsp hot water
4 oz (110 g) icing sugar

Preheat the oven to 350°F/180°C/Gas Mk 4. Grease and line an 8 inch (20 cm) sandwich tin. Put the margarine, sugar, eggs, flour and 3 tbsp marmalade in a bowl and add the hot water. Beat well for 2-3 minutes until evenly blended. Spoon into the tin and bake for 35-40 minutes, or until a skewer inserted comes out clean. Turn out onto a wire rack to cool. Remove the lining paper. If desired the cake can be spread with a little marmalade and coated with a glacé icing.

PINEAPPLE UPSIDE-DOWN CAKE
Makes an 8 inch (20 cm) cake

Use recipe for Victoria sponge 1 on page 25

Topping:
1 can pineapple rings
2-3 tbsp demerara sugar
1 tbsp softened butter

Preheat the oven to 375°F/190°C/Gas Mk 5. Make the cake as directed on page 25. Coat an 8 inch (20 cm) loose-bottomed cake tin with softened butter and sprinkle all over with demerara sugar. Stand on a baking tray. Place drained tinned pineapple rings on the sugared base and cover with the sponge mixture. Bake in centre of the oven for 35-45 minutes. Turn out while hot and serve with cream as a dessert or eat cold as a cake.

MARBLE CAKE
Makes a 2 lb (1 kg) loaf or a 7 inch (18 cm) deep square cake

6 oz (175 g) soft margarine
6 oz (175 g) caster sugar
2 eggs, beaten
6 oz (175 g) self-raising flour

1½ tsp baking powder
2 tsp cocoa powder
2 tsp warm water
pink food colouring

Icing: 3 oz (75 g) soft margarine
8 oz (225 g) icing sugar, sifted with 1 tbsp cocoa powder
1 tbsp warm water
1 tbsp milk
chopped nuts to decorate

Preheat the oven to 325°F/160°C/Gas Mk 3. Place all cake ingredients in a bowl and beat well with a wooden spoon for about 3 minutes. Divide into three. To one third add 2 tsp cocoa blended with the 2 tsp warm water and mix well. Colour one third with pink food colouring and leave the remaining third plain. Grease and base line a 2 lb (1 kg) loaf tin and spoon in alternate spoonfuls of the coloured mixtures and gently swirl around with a skewer. Bake in the centre of the oven for 1¼ - 1½ hours until firm to the touch. Turn out, remove the lining paper and leave to cool on a wire tray. Place all the icing ingredients in a bowl and beat together until smooth. Spread around the sides and top of the cake. Cover the sides with chopped nuts. Pipe icing along the sides at the top of the cake and swirl the flat iced area with a fork.

BANANA UPSIDE-DOWN CAKE
Makes an 8 inch (20 cm) cake

Use recipe for Victoria sponge 1 on page 25

Topping:
2 bananas, sliced
2-3 tbsp demerara sugar
1 tbsp softened butter
a little lemon juice

Preheat the oven to 375°F/190°C/Gas Mk 5. Make the cake as directed on page 25. Coat an 8 inch (20 cm) loose-bottomed cake tin with softened butter and sprinkle all over with demerara sugar. Stand on a baking tray. Place the sliced bananas on the sugared base and sprinkle with lemon juice. Cover with cake mixture. Bake in centre of the oven for 30 minutes. Turn out while hot and serve with cream. Eat cold as a cake if preferred.

SYRUPY YOGHURT CAKE
Makes a slab cake

4 oz (110 g) butter
1 lb (450 g) caster sugar
2 eggs
10 oz (300 g) self-raising flour

½ tsp baking powder
½ pt (300 ml) yoghurt
pinch salt

Syrup: 1½ pt (900 ml) water, boiled for 10 minutes
with 10 oz (300 g) sugar

Preheat the oven 375°F/190°C/Gas Mk 5. Cream the butter and sugar together until light and fluffy, then beat in the eggs one at a time. Sift the flour, baking powder and salt together and fold into the creamed mixture, alternately with the yoghurt. Grease and line a 10 x 14 inch (25 x 35 cm) roasting tin and pour in the mixture. Bake in the centre of the oven for 30-40 minutes, or until the cake is cooked through and a thin skewer inserted into the centre comes out clean. Let it cool for a few minutes before removing from the tin and cooling on a rack. Place on the serving plate and pour over the syrup. This cake can be varied by adding the grated rind of 1 lemon to the mixture and separating the whites from the yolks of the eggs and adding them, stiffly whisked, before pouring into the cake tin. Bake as before.

MADEIRA CAKE
Makes a 10 inch (25 cm) cake

8 oz (225 g) butter or margarine
8 oz (225 g) caster sugar
4 eggs
12 oz (350 g) plain flour, sifted

pinch of salt
2 tsp baking powder
grated rind of 1 lemon
milk to mix

Preheat the oven to 350°F/170°C/Gas Mk 4. Grease and line a 10 inch (25 cm) cake tin. Cream the softened butter or margarine with the caster sugar and grated lemon rind until very soft and fluffy. Beat the eggs together lightly and gradually beat into the mixture a little at a time. A little of the sieved flour can be added if the mixture begins to curdle. Sift the flour again with the salt and baking powder then fold lightly into the creamed mixture with a metal spoon, adding a little milk if necessary to obtain a smooth, fairly stiff dropping consistency. Bake for 1-1¼ hours.

TURKISH HALVA CAKE
Makes a 10 portion ring cake

4 oz (110 g) butter
4 oz (110 g) caster sugar
2 oranges
2 eggs, beaten

6 oz (175 g) semolina
2 level tsp baking powder
2 oz (50 g) ground almonds

Syrup: 10 oz (300 g) caster sugar
pinch of ground cinnamon
2 oz (50 g) candied peel

¼ pt (150 ml) water
¼ pt (150 ml) orange juice

Preheat the oven to 425°F/220°C/Gas Mk 7. Butter a 2 pt (1 litre) ring mould. Beat butter and sugar together until light and fluffy in colour and texture. Then beat in the finely grated rind and 4 tbsp of juice from one orange. Add the eggs, semolina and baking powder sifted together, and the ground almonds. Stir together then turn into the mould and bake in centre of oven for 10 minutes. Turn down heat to moderate (350°F/180°C/Gas Mk 4) and bake for a further 25 minutes or until lightly golden and firm to touch. Leave in tin. Heat the water and sugar in a small saucepan until completely dissolved. Add the remaining ingredients, except the peel and bring to the boil. Boil gently for 4 minutes then add peel. Remove cake from tin whilst it is still warm and pour the syrup over immediately.

GENOESE SPONGE
Makes a 7 inch (18 cm) deep sandwich cake

2 oz (50 g) softened butter
2 tbsp hot water
3 eggs
3 oz (75 g) caster sugar
4 oz (110 g) self-raising flour, sifted

Preheat the oven to 375°F/190°C/Gas Mk 5. Butter and flour two
sandwich cake tins. Put the butter and water in a small saucepan over
a gentle heat to melt, and then allow to cool. Whisk the eggs and
sugar together with an electric whisk until foamy. Stir the butter mixture into the egg mixture. Sift the flour into the mixture a little at a
time, folding it in very carefully with a metal spoon. Pour into the tins
and bake in the centre of the oven for about 20 minutes or until
golden and firm to the touch.

GERMAN COFFEE CAKE
Makes an 8 portion ring cake

6 oz (175 g) margarine
6 oz (175 g) caster sugar
3 eggs

6 oz (175 g) self-raising flour, sifted
pinch of salt
4 level tbsp coffee essence

Syrup: 1 level tbsp dark brown sugar
½ pint (300 ml) boiling water
2 tbsp rum, optional

Grease and flour a ½ pint (300 ml) ring mould. Preheat the oven to
375°F/190°C/Gas Mk 5. Beat the margarine and caster sugar together
until light and fluffy in colour and texture. Add the eggs, one at a
time, beating well after each addition, adding a little flour if the mixture curdles. Gently fold in the sifted flour and salt with a metal
spoon. Turn the mixture into the mould and level the top with the
back of a spoon. Bake for 30 minutes or until springy to the touch
and cooked through. Leave to cool in the tin for 5 minutes then turn
out onto a wire rack. Blend the coffee essence with the brown sugar
and water in a saucepan over a low heat, remove when sugar is
melted, add rum (if using) and leave to cool. Stand the cake on a large
plate and slowly pour over the coffee liquid, making sure the entire
cake surface is moistened. Leave for 2 hours to allow the cake to soak
up the coffee.

CHOCOLATE OIL CAKE
Makes a 7 inch (18 cm) sandwich cake

6 oz (175 g) flour
2 tbsp cocoa powder
1 tsp bicarbonate of soda
1 tsp baking powder
5 oz (150 g) caster sugar

2 tbsp black treacle
2 eggs
5 fl oz (150 ml) sunflower oil
5 fl oz (150 ml) milk

Preheat the oven to 325°F/170°C/Gas Mk 3. Sift the flour, cocoa, bicarbonate of soda and baking powder together and stir in the sugar. Pour the treacle, beaten eggs, oil and milk onto the flour mixture and beat until thoroughly blended. Divide the batter between two greased and floured 7 inch (18 cm) sandwich tins and bake in the centre of the oven for 40 minutes until the cake springs back when gently pressed. Remove from the oven and leave in the tins for 5 minutes before turning out onto a wire tray and leaving to cool. When cold sandwich together with chocolate butter icing.

FROSTED COFFEE MARBLE CAKE
Makes a deep 7 inch (18 cm) cake

6 oz (175 g) soft margarine
6 oz (175 g) caster sugar
6 oz (175 g) self-raising flour, sifted
1 rounded tsp baking powder

3 eggs
1 tbsp instant coffee, blended
  with 1 tbsp hot water, cooled

Frosting:
3 oz (75 g) butter
3 tsp instant coffee
9 oz (250 g) icing sugar, sifted

3 oz (75 g) soft brown sugar
2½ tbsp milk
10 coffee beans to decorate

Preheat the oven to 375°F/190°C/Gas Mk 5. Grease and base line two 7 inch (18 cm) sandwich tins. In a bowl beat together all the cake ingredients, except the coffee, until well mixed. Using half the mixture, dot teaspoonfuls over the prepared tins. Beat coffee into remaining cake mixture, then spoon between plain mixture. Smooth the top of each cake. Bake for 25-30 minutes and cool on a wire rack then remove the paper. To make the frosting, melt the butter, sugar and coffee in a pan and bring to the boil slowly, stirring. Remove from heat, add milk and beat in icing sugar until the frosting is smooth and quite thick. Cover with clingfilm and allow to cool. Place frosting in a piping bag fitted with large star tube. Turn one cake upside-down so that the marbling shows and pipe 10 rosettes, equally spaced, around the edge. Sandwich cake with remaining frosting.

COCONUT CAKE
Makes a 10 inch (25 cm) deep cake

8 oz (225 g) butter or soft margarine
8 oz (225 g) caster sugar
4 eggs, beaten
12 oz (350 g) plain flour, sifted
pinch of salt

2 tsp baking powder
4 oz (110 g) desiccated coconut
few drops vanilla essence
milk to mix

Preheat the oven to 350°F/180°C/Gas Mk 4. Grease and line a 10 inch (25 cm) round cake tin. Cream the softened butter or margarine with the caster sugar until very soft and pale. Gradually beat the eggs into the mixture a little at a time. A little flour can be added if the mixture curdles. Sift the flour, salt and baking powder together and fold gently into the creamed mixture with a metal spoon. Add the desiccated coconut and vanilla essence and stir, adding milk if necessary to obtain a smooth, fairly stiff dropping consistency. Bake for 1-1¼ hours.

GINGER CAKE

4 oz (110 g) preserved ginger
4 oz (110 g) butter
3 oz (75 g) golden syrup
1 oz (25 g) black treacle
4 oz (110 g) soft brown sugar
½ tsp bicarbonate of soda

4 tbsp milk
8 oz (225 g) plain flour, sifted
1 tsp ground ginger
pinch of salt
1 egg

Preheat the oven to 325°F/170°C/Gas Mk 3. Chop the preserved ginger and grease and line the bottom of a large Swiss roll tin. Melt the butter, golden syrup, black treacle and sugar in a saucepan without boiling and when the sugar has dissolved add the ginger and allow to cool. Mix the bicarbonate of soda with 1 tbsp milk. Sift the flour into a bowl together with the salt and ground ginger and make a well in the centre. Break the egg and remaining 3 tbsp milk into the treacle mixture and slowly beat into the flour then stir in the bicarbonate of soda and milk. Turn into a lined and greased shallow rectangular tin and bake for about 1 hour. The cake should be moist and slightly sticky but use a warm skewer to check that the middle is cooked. Cool in the tin before turning out.

OLD FASHIONED SEED CAKE
Makes a 7 inch (18 cm) deep round cake

10 oz (300 g) self-raising flour, sifted
5 oz (150 g) butter or soft margarine
5 oz (150 g) caster sugar
1 oz (25 g) caraway seeds
2 oz (50 g) mixed peel (optional)

1 small lemon
pinch freshly grated nutmeg
2 eggs
5-6 tbsp milk
demerara sugar for sprinkling

Preheat the oven to 375°F/190°C/Gas Mk 5. Grease and line 7 inch (18 cm) round cake tin. Sift the flour into a mixing bowl and rub in the butter or margarine until the mixture resembles fine breadcrumbs. Stir in the caraway seeds, sugar and mixed peel (if using). Grate the lemon rind and add to the mixture with the grated nutmeg. Beat the eggs and milk together lightly and mix into the flour mixture. Stir until a soft dropping consistency is achieved, adding more milk if necessary. Turn into the tin and bake on the lower centre shelf of the oven for 1-1¼ hours until the cake is golden brown and springy to the touch. Turn out onto a wire rack to cool and remove the greaseproof paper Sprinkle with demerara sugar and leave cool.

SNOW WHITE CAKE
Makes a 7 inch (18 cm) deep square cake

4 oz (110 g) self-raising flour, sifted
10 oz (300 g) cornflour
½ level tsp salt
10 oz (300 g) caster sugar
grated rind of 1 lemon

7 fl oz (200 ml) corn oil
7 fl oz (200 ml) water
¼ tsp vanilla essence
4 large egg whites

Preheat the oven to 325°F/170°C/ Gas Mk 3. Grease and line a 7 inch (18 cm) deep square cake tin. Sift the self-raising flour and cornflour together with the salt into a large mixing bowl. Stir in the sugar and lemon rind and make a well in the centre. Mix the oil and water together with the vanilla essence and pour gently into the well in the centre of the flour, stir in evenly with a wooden spoon. When the batter is smooth beat well for about 1 minute. Whisk the egg whites until they are stiff and then fold them lightly into the batter mix with a metal spoon. Pour into the prepared tin and bake in the centre of the oven for about 1½ hours or until it is firm to the touch and just shrinking away from the edge of the tin. Turn onto a wire tray to cool. To keep for a week or so, wrap in greaseproof paper and foil when cold.

GRANDMA'S GINGERBREAD
Makes a 7 inch (18 cm) square tin

8 oz (225 g) self-raising flour, sifted
2 oz (50 g) soft brown sugar
1 tsp ground ginger
1 tsp mixed spice
1 tsp bicarbonate of soda

4 oz (110 g) margarine
4 oz (110 g) black treacle
4 oz (110 g) golden syrup
1 egg
¼pt (150 ml) milk

Preheat the oven to 375°F/190°C/Gas Mk 5. Grease and line a 7 inch (18 cm) square tin. Sift the flour, spices and bicarbonate of soda together into a mixing bowl with the sugar. Melt the margarine, treacle and golden syrup in a small saucepan. Beat the egg and milk together and tip into the treacle mixture when it comes off the heat. Stir quickly into the dry ingredients and mix. Pour into the tin and bake for 45 minutes until firm on top.

MOCHA CAKE
Makes a 7 inch deep sandwich cake

5 oz (150 g) light soft brown sugar
5 oz (150 g) plain flour, sifted
2 level tsp baking powder
½ level tsp salt
3½ fl oz (100 ml) corn oil

3 ½ fl oz (100 ml) milk
1 tbsp coffee essence
few drops almond essence
2 large eggs, separated
2 oz (50 g) chocolate polka dots

Coffee Butter Icing:
10 oz (300 g) icing sugar
5 oz (150 g) butter or margarine
1-1½ tbsp coffee essence
1 tbsp hot water

Preheat the oven to 400°F/200°C/Gas Mk 6. Grease and lightly flour two 7 inch (18 cm) sandwich tins. Stir the sugar into the flour, baking powder and salt. Blend the corn oil, milk, coffee and almond essence together. Separate the eggs and add the yolks to the oil and milk mixture. Pour this mixture into the dry ingredients and beat well to form a smooth batter. Whisk the egg whites until stiff and carefully fold into the cake batter. Fold in the polka dots. Divide the mixture between the sandwich tins and bake for 15-20 minutes. Cool on a wire rack. Prepare the coffee butter icing by creaming the butter or margarine until it is light and soft, and gradually sift in the icing sugar. Add the coffee essence and hot water and mix well. Sandwich the cold cakes together with butter icing and coat the top and sides, swirling the icing round for a rippled effect.

CHOCOLATE LAYER SQUARES
Makes 16 squares

Sponge:	*1½ oz (40 g) plain chocolate* *3 oz (75 g) butter* *2 oz (50 g) caster sugar* *2 large eggs* *8 oz (225 g) plain flour* *pinch of salt*
Filling:	*2 level tbsp custard powder* *½ pt (300 ml) milk* *3 oz (75 g) butter* *few drops of rum essence* *4 oz (110 g) sifted icing sugar* *1 oz (25 g) cocoa powder*
Topping:	*2½ oz (60 g) plain chocolate* *½ oz (10 g) caster sugar* *1 tbsp water* *½ tsp cooking oil*

Preheat the oven to 350°F/180°C/Gas Mk 4. Grease and line a large Swiss roll tin. Melt the chocolate in a bowl standing over hot water. Beat the softened butter and caster sugar to a soft fluffy mixture and then beat in the melted chocolate. Separate the eggs and beat the yolks into the mixture. Sift the flour and salt together; whisk the egg whites until they are very stiff and then fold these two alternately into the mixture with a metal spoon. Turn the mixture into the tin and spread over evenly. Bake on the centre shelf of the oven for 15-20 minutes or until the cake is cooked. Loosen the sides away from the tin with a palette knife and turn onto a wire rack. Peel off the lining paper and leave to cool. To make the filling, mix the custard powder with a little of the cold milk then blend in the rest of the milk, bring to the boil stirring all the time until it thickens. Remove from the heat and beat in the butter and rum essence. Leave to cool with a piece of clingfilm covering the top of the custard to prevent a skin from forming. When the mixture is cool gradually beat in the sifted icing sugar and cocoa powder and then leave to cool completely. When both cake and filling are cold, split the cake in half and sandwich together with the filling. To make the topping, break the chocolate into a saucepan, add the sugar, water and oil and stir over a very low heat until all the ingredients are melted and blended. Leave to cool and thicken and then spread over the top of the cake. When the icing is set the cake can be cut into 16 squares.

CHOCOHOLIC'S DELIGHT

4 oz (110 g) butter
2 oz (50 g) plain chocolate
2 eggs
½ tsp vanilla essence
8 oz (225 g) granulated sugar
2 oz (50 g) plain flour

¼ level tsp baking powder
½ level tsp salt
1½ oz (40 g) packet mixed
    nuts and raisins
2 oz (50 g) desiccated coconut

Topping:
2 Mars bars
2 oz (50 g) butter

1 tbsp golden syrup
2 oz (50 g) icing sugar, sifted

Preheat the oven to 350°F/180°C/Gas Mk 4. Line a Swiss roll tin with foil and brush with oil. Melt the butter and broken up chocolate gently in a medium sized saucepan until completely dissolved. Remove the pan from the heat. Beat in the eggs, one at a time, until the mixture thickens. Beat in the vanilla essence and stir in the granulated sugar. Mix the flour, baking powder, salt, nuts, raisins and coconut together in a bowl, then add to the chocolate mixture and beat with a wooden spoon until thoroughly mixed. Pour the mixture into the tin and bake just above the centre of the oven for 50-60 minutes until firm to the touch and the cake has shrunk away from the sides of the tin. Leave to cool in the tin for 5 minutes, then turn out onto a wire rack to cool. Peel off the foil. Roughly chop the Mars bars and put in a saucepan with the butter and golden syrup. Cook over a gentle heat, stirring, until mixture becomes fudge-like, then beat in the icing sugar until smooth and pour over the cold cake. As the topping cools, mark the top with a fork and leave to set before cutting into 20 squares.

GOLDEN SPONGE

2 oz (50 g) butter
2 oz (50 g) sugar
4 tbsp golden syrup

1 egg
2 tbsp milk
4 oz (110 g) self-raising flour

Preheat the oven to 350°F/180°C/Gas Mk 4. Melt together the butter, sugar and syrup over low heat until the butter has just melted, then cool slightly. Beat together the egg and milk. Add the egg mixture and flour alternately to the melted butter. Mix well and pour into a greased 8 inch (20 cm) sandwich tin. Bake in the oven for 35 minutes. Cool on a wire rack. This cake can be iced if desired.

MUM'S PARKIN
Makes a 7 inch (18 cm) square cake

8 oz (225 g) plain flour, sifted
4 oz (110 g) medium oatmeal
4 oz (110 g) soft brown sugar
½ tsp ground ginger
10 oz (300 g) golden syrup

3 oz (75 g) margarine
¼ pt (150 ml) milk (or less)
pinch of salt
1 tsp bicarbonate of soda

Preheat the oven to 300°F/150°C/Gas Mk 2. Grease and line a 7 inch (18 cm) square tin. Mix the sifted flour with the oatmeal and ginger in a large mixing bowl. Melt together the sugar, margarine, syrup and a little of the milk. Dissolve the bicarbonate of soda in 1 tbsp of milk. Pour the melted sugar mixture into the flour and add the dissolved bicarbonate of soda. Beat well and pour into the tin. Bake for 1¼ hours or until firm to the touch.

RIBBON LAYER CAKE
Makes a 7inch (18 cm) deep cake

6 oz (175 g) soft margarine
6 oz (175 g) caster sugar
3 large eggs

6 oz (175 g) self-raising flour, sifted
1½ level tsp baking powder
pink and green food colouring

Icing:
3 oz (75 g) soft margarine
2 tbsp milk; desiccated coconut

8 oz (225 g) icing sugar, sifted
coloured jelly sweets to decorate

Preheat the oven to 325°F/170°C/Gas Mk 3. Grease and flour three 7 inch (18 cm) sandwich tins. Cream the margarine with the caster sugar until soft and fluffy. Beat in the eggs one at a time and then fold in the flour and baking powder sieved together. Divide the mixture into three. Stir enough pink colouring to make a gentle shade of pink into one third of the mixture, green colouring into the second third and leave the remainder plain. Place the three mixtures in the tins, and bake in the centre of the oven for about 35 minutes or until firm to the touch. Turn out onto wire trays and leave to cool. For the icing, cream the margarine and icing sugar together until soft and add the vanilla essence. Sandwich the three cakes together with the icing, spread a thin layer of icing round the sides of the cake and roll in desiccated coconut. Spread the rest of the icing on the top of the cake. Mark in swirls with a fork and pipe round the edges. Decorate with the coloured jelly sweets.

VANILLA SQUARE
Makes an 8 inch (20 cm) square cake

3 oz (75 g) margarine
3 oz (75g) caster sugar
2 large eggs
3 oz (75 g) plain flour
2 oz (50 g) cornflour
pinch of salt

½ level tsp cream of tartar
½ level tsp bicarbonate of soda
½ level tsp vanilla essence
3 tbsp milk
4 level tbsp sifted icing sugar

Preheat the oven to 350°F/180°C/Gas Mk 4. Grease a shallow 8 inch (20 cm) square cake tin and line the base with greaseproof paper. Cream together the margarine and sugar until they are light and fluffy. Beat the eggs and gradually stir them into the creamed mixture. Sift together the flour, cornflour, salt, cream of tartar and bicarbonate of soda and fold them into the mixture with the vanilla essence and the milk. Turn into the prepared tin and level the top. Bake on the centre shelf of the oven for 40 minutes or until the cake is springy to the touch. Cool in the tin for about 15 minutes before turning out onto a wire tray.

CHOCOLATE BRANDY CAKE
Makes 12 slices

8 oz (225 g) digestive biscuits
8 oz (225 g) plain chocolate
8 oz (225 g) butter
2 eggs

3 oz (75 g) caster sugar
2 oz (50 g) glacé cherries
2 oz (50 g) walnut pieces
2 tbsp brandy or rum

Crush the digestive biscuits coarsely in a plastic bag or in a food processor and set them aside. Grease a loose-bottomed 7 inch (18 cm) flan or cake tin and line with a strip of lightly oiled foil. Melt the chocolate with the butter in a bowl placed over boiling water, remove from the heat and leave to cool slightly. Beat the eggs and sugar together until they are thick and creamy and then beat in the cooled chocolate and butter. Fold in three-quarters of the glacé cherries and walnuts, the brandy and the crushed biscuits. Press into the tin. Decorate with the remaining cherries and walnuts and store in the refrigerator until about ½ hour before serving. Run a sharp knife around the edge of the cake and push up the base. It is best to leave the cake on this when cutting into slices. Serve in small slices, as it is very rich.

SPICY HONEY CAKE
Makes a 2 lb (1 kg) cake

10 oz (300 g) plain flour, sifted
pinch of salt
½ level tsp ground ginger
3 oz (75 g) caster sugar
1 level tsp bicarbonate of soda
¼pt (150 ml) milk
5 oz (150 g) clear honey
1 oz (25 g) butter or soft margarine

Preheat the oven to 350°F/180°C/Gas Mk 4. Sift the flour, salt and ginger into a mixing bowl and add the caster sugar. Dissolve the bicarbonate of soda in 2 tbsp of the milk in a small cup. Put the rest of the milk in a small saucepan together with the honey and butter or margarine and heat gently until melted. Remove from the heat. Stir the bicarbonate of soda and the milk into the centre of the dry ingredients, add the milk and honey liquid and stir round. Beat all the ingredients together until the mixture is smooth. Pour into a greased medium-sized loaf tin, level the surface and bake in the centre of the oven for 20 minutes. Reduce the temperature to 325°F/170°C/Gas Mk 3 and continue cooking for a further 40 minutes or until firm to the touch. Turn out onto a wire rack to cool.

CHOCOLATE POLKA DOT CAKE
Makes a 7 inch (18 cm) deep round cake

2 oz (50 g) margarine
4 oz (110 g) light soft brown sugar
1 large egg
5 oz (150 g) plain flour

½ oz (10 g) cocoa powder
½ level tsp bicarbonate of soda
¼pint (150 ml) milk
1 oz (25 g) chocolate polka dots

Preheat the oven to 350°F/180°C/Gas Mk 4. Grease a 7 inch (18 cm) deep round cake tin and line with greaseproof paper. Separate the egg. Cream together the margarine and brown sugar until they are light and fluffy, then beat in the egg yolk. Sift the flour, cocoa and bicarbonate of soda together and lightly fold them into the creamed mixture with the milk. Stir in the polka dots. Whisk the egg white until it forms stiff peaks, then carefully fold it into the mixture. Turn into the tin and make a hollow in the centre, so that the cake rises evenly. Bake for about 1 hour on the centre shelf of the oven, or until a skewer inserted into the cake comes out clean.

RUM CAKE
Makes an 8 inch (20 cm) sandwich cake

4 oz (110 g) self-raising flour
½ tsp bicarbonate of soda
1½ oz (40 g) cocoa powder
6 tbsp cold water
3 tbsp dark rum
4 oz (110 g) butter
8 oz (225 g) caster sugar
2 eggs
2 oz (50 g) ground almonds

Preheat the oven to 325°F/170°C/Gas Mk 3. Line and grease an 8 inch (20 cm) deep sandwich tin. Sift together the flour, bicarbonate of soda and cocoa powder into a bowl and stir in the water and rum. Cream the butter and sugar together until light and fluffy and gradually beat in the eggs, a little at a time. Carefully fold in the ground almonds, using a metal spoon, and then the flour and cocoa mixture alternately. Turn into the tin and bake in the centre of the oven for about 1 hour, or until the cake is springy to the touch. Leave in the tin for 5 minutes before turning out onto a wire rack to cool.

AUNT BELLE'S PARKIN
Makes 16 squares

3 oz (75 g) golden syrup
1 oz (25 g) treacle
4 oz (110 g) soft brown sugar
4 oz (110 g) butter
6 oz (175 g) self-raising flour, sifted
6 oz (175 g) medium oatmeal

2 level tsp ground ginger
pinch of salt
1 egg beaten
4 fl oz (125 ml) milk
½ tsp bicarbonate of soda
extra egg to glaze (optional)

Preheat the oven to 350°F/180°C/Gas Mk 4. Melt the syrup, treacle, sugar and butter together in a saucepan, stirring gently until dissolved. Mix the dry ingredients together in a bowl and pour on the treacle mixture. Beat the eggs and milk and add the bicarbonate of soda then blend this into the mixture in the bowl. Pour into a well greased large Swiss roll tin and brush the top with beaten egg. Bake for 1 hour or until firm. This cake is better eaten after standing, well wrapped, for a couple of days.

CHEQUERBOARD CAKE
Makes a 7 inch (18 cm) deep sandwich cake

6 oz (175 g) soft margarine
6 oz (175 g) caster sugar
3 large eggs
6 oz (175 g) self-raising flour, sifted
1½ level tsp baking powder
1 level tbsp cocoa powder
2 tbsp water
2 tbsp apricot jam, warmed and sieved

Icing:
3 oz (75 g) soft margarine
8 oz (225 g) icing sugar, sifted
1 level tbsp cocoa powder
1 tbsp water
chocolate vermicelli to decorate

Preheat the oven to 325°F/170°C/Gas Mk 3. Cream the margarine with the caster sugar until soft and fluffy. Beat in the eggs one at a time and then fold in the sifted flour and baking powder. Divide the mixture in half. To one half add 1 tbsp cocoa powder mixed with 2 tbsp water. Place the two mixtures in two greased and floured 7 inch (18 cm) sandwich tins, and bake in the centre of the oven for about 35 minutes or until firm to the touch. Turn out onto wire trays and leave to cool. Using 4 inch (10 cm) and 1 inch (2½ cm) round cutters cut each cake into 3 rounds. Brush joins with the warmed and sieved apricot jam and replace the middle sized ring on the vanilla cake with the chocolate ring and the plain ring between the two chocolate pieces. Sandwich the two cakes together with apricot jam. For the icing, cream the margarine and icing sugar together until soft. Divide the icing in two and then beat the cocoa powder mixed with the water into one half. Spread a thin layer of chocolate icing round the sides of the cake and roll in chocolate vermicelli. Pipe the rest of the icing in alternate plain and chocolate triangles round the top of the cake.

CHOCOLATE FUDGE CAKE
Makes an 11 x 7 inch (28 x 18 cm) slab cake

8 oz (225 g) plain flour ,sifted
2 level tbsp cocoa powder
1 level tsp baking powder
½ level tsp bicarbonate of soda
2 oz (50 g) plain chocolate
4 oz (110 g) butter or margarine
6 oz (175 g) soft light brown sugar
1 large egg
¼ pt (150 ml) natural yoghurt
½ tsp vanilla essence
water

Icing:
3 oz (75 g) butter
5 oz (150 g) icing sugar, sifted
2 level tbsp cocoa powder
2 oz (50 g) plain chocolate, melted

Preheat the oven to 375°F/190°C/Gas Mk 5. Grease and fully line a Swiss roll tin, making sure the greaseproof paper comes 1 inch (2.5 cm) above the rim of the tin. Melt the chocolate gently in a saucepan with 2 tbsp water, then bring to the boil and allow to cool. Cream the butter and sugar together until light and fluffy in colour and texture, then beat in the egg. Fold in the cooled chocolate, yoghurt and vanilla essence. Sift the flour, cocoa powder, bicarbonate of soda and salt together and fold into the creamed mixture gently with a metal spoon. Spoon into the tin and bake in the centre of the oven for 1 hour or until a warm skewer inserted into the cake comes out clean. Leave in the tin for 10 minutes and then turn out onto a wire tray to cool. Remove the lining paper. To make the frosting, cream the butter and icing sugar together, beat in the cocoa powder and then the 2 oz (50 g) melted plain chocolate and leave to cool. Top the cake with the frosting and decorate with chopped walnuts.

SMALL CAKES

ICED CHERRY CAKES
Makes 20

6 oz (175 g) self-raising flour, sifted
4 oz (110 g) soft margarine
4 oz (110 g) caster sugar
2 eggs
¼ tsp almond essence
2 oz (50 g) glacé cherries, washed, chopped and floured

Decoration: 6 oz (175 g) icing sugar;
8-10 glacé cherries; a few toasted flaked almonds

Preheat the oven to 375°F/190°C/Gas Mk 5. Put all cake ingredients into a large bowl and beat with a wooden spoon for 3 minutes until well mixed, or beat for 2 minutes with an electric mixer. Spoon the mixture into about 20 paper cake cases placed on a baking tray, filling the cases about two-thirds full. Bake for 15-20 minutes or until firm to the touch. Mix the icing sugar with water until a stiff consistency is obtained. When the cakes are cold, spread them with the icing and decorate with cherries and flaked almonds.

GRANNY'S ROCK CAKES
Makes about 12

8 oz (225 g) self-raising flour, sifted
4 oz (110 g) margarine, cubed
3 oz (75 g) granulated sugar
3 oz (75 g) cleaned sultanas
1 oz (25 g) chopped mixed peel
1 large egg
1-2 tbsp milk

Preheat the oven to 400°F/200°C/Gas Mk 6. Sift the flour into a mixing bowl and rub in the margarine until the mixture resembles fine breadcrumbs. Stir in the sugar, sultanas and chopped peel and then bind together with the egg and enough milk to make a stiff consistency. Place dessertspoonfuls of the mixture onto greased baking trays, allowing space for them to spread during cooking. Bake for about 15 minutes or until they are golden brown and firm. Leave to cool on a wire tray.

STICKY GINGER MADELEINES
Makes 18

8 oz (225 g) plain flour, sifted
2 level tsp ground ginger
½ level tsp mixed spice
3 oz (75 g) sultanas
2 oz (50 g) soft brown sugar

8 level tbsp golden syrup
4 oz (110 g) margarine
¼ pint (150 ml) milk
1 level tsp bicarbonate of soda
1 egg, beaten

Glaze: 8 level tbsp jelly or sieved marmalade
         1 tbsp lemon juice
         preserved ginger, cut into 18 pieces

Grease 18 dariole moulds or bun tins and preheat the oven to
350°F/180°C/Gas Mk 4. Sift the flour and spices into a mixing bowl,
then stir in the sultanas and sugar. Place the syrup and margarine in a
pan and melt gently. Warm the milk and stir in the bicarbonate of
soda. Add the syrup mixture to the milk, then add to the dry ingredients, alternating with the beaten egg, and, once all the ingredients have
been added, beat until smooth. Pour 2 tablespoons of the mixture into
each mould and bake for 35 minutes. Leave in the tins to cool.
Meanwhile gently warm the marmalade and lemon juice together in a
small pan over a gentle heat until melted. Brush each cake with the
glaze and then place a piece of ginger on top to finish. Serve the cakes
in paper cases, as they are sticky to handle.

STRAWBERRY BUNS
Makes 16

8 oz (225 g) self-raising flour, sifted
4 oz (110 g) soft margarine, cubed
3 oz (75 g) granulated sugar
1 large egg, beaten

2 tbsp milk
2 level tbsp strawberry jam
little extra caster sugar and milk
   for glaze

Preheat the oven to 400°F/200°C/Gas Mk 6. Sift the flour into a mixing bowl and add the margarine. Rub in the margarine until the mixture resembles fine breadcrumbs. Stir in the sugar and then bind
together with the beaten egg and milk to make a fairly stiff mixture.
Knead the mixture lightly on a floured board, and cut into sixteen
pieces. Roll into small balls in floured hands and lay them on greased
baking trays. Make a hollow in the top of each bun and put in a small
spoonful of jam - not too much or it will run out and burn during
cooking. Brush the surface of the buns with a little milk and sprinkle
with caster sugar. Bake in the oven for 12-15 minutes until golden
brown. Cool on a wire tray.

ORANGE AND COCONUT FLAPJACKS
Makes 16

7 oz (200 g) butter
2 oz (50 g) golden syrup
4 oz (110 g) muscovado sugar

grated rind of 1 orange
8 oz (225 g) porridge oats
2 oz (50 g) desiccated coconut

Preheat the oven to 350°F/180°C/Gas Mk 4. Melt the butter and syrup together in a large saucepan. Remove from the heat and stir in the sugar, orange rind, porridge oats and desiccated coconut. Grease a Swiss roll tin and press the mixture into the tin evenly. Bake for about 15 minutes until golden brown. Allow to cool slightly, then cut into fingers and carefully place on a wire tray to cool completely.

ORANGE CHOCOLATE SLICES
Makes 16 slices

4 oz (110 g) margarine
4 oz (110 g) caster sugar
4 oz (110 g) self-raising flour, sifted
½ level tsp baking powder

2 eggs, beaten
finely grated rind of ½ orange
1 level tbsp cocoa
1 tsp water

Icing:
8 oz (225 g) icing sugar
1-2 tsp orange juice
1 level tbsp cocoa powder

Preheat the oven to 375°F/190°C/Gas Mk 5. Mix together the margarine, sugar, flour, baking powder and eggs until the mixture is light and fluffy. Divide the mixture in two, add the orange rind to one half and stir thoroughly. Sift the cocoa powder into the other half, add a teaspoon of water and mix well. Place heaped teaspoonfuls of the orange mixture randomly over the base of the tin, with heaped teaspoonfuls of the cocoa mixture in between. Smooth the top. Cook in the centre of the oven for 25-35 minutes. Turn out and cool on a wire tray. To make the icing, sift 6 oz (175 g) of the icing sugar into a bowl with the cocoa. Add enough water to make a rather thick coating consistency. Sift the 2 oz (50 g) of icing sugar into another bowl and add enough orange juice to make this icing a slightly thinner consistency. Pour the chocolate icing on top of the cake and smooth with a flat knife. Decoratively pipe the orange icing over the top. Allow to set before cutting into fingers.

MADELEINES
Makes 12

4 oz (110 g) soft margarine
4 oz (110 g) caster sugar
2 large eggs, beaten
4 oz (110 g) self-raising flour
pinch of salt

1 tbsp milk
8 oz (225 g) raspberry jam, warmed
  and sieved
2 oz (50 g) desiccated coconut
6 glacé cherries, halved

Preheat the oven to 375°F/190°C/Gas Mk 5. Cream the margarine and sugar together until light and fluffy in colour and texture. Add the eggs gradually to the creamed mixture, beating well between each addition. If the mixture begins to curdle, add a little of the flour. Sift the flour and salt together then fold lightly into the creamed mixture using a metal spoon, adding more milk if necessary to obtain a soft dropping consistency. Brush 12 dariole moulds with melted fat and divide the mixture evenly between them, only filling the moulds half-way up, to allow the cakes to rise. Bake in the centre of the oven for about 20 minutes or until they are well risen, golden brown and firm to the touch. Carefully remove from the moulds, loosening with a knife, and leave to cool on a wire tray. When the cakes are cold trim the bases so that they stand level. Hold each Madeleine on a fork and brush the sides and top of each cake with the warmed and sieved raspberry jam, then roll in the desiccated coconut. Top each Madeleine with half a glacé cherry.

CRISPY DATE TRIANGLES
Makes 9

2 oz (50 g) margarine
4 oz (110 g) caster sugar
8 oz (225 g) dates, stoned and chopped
1 oz (25 g) glacé cherries, quartered

1 oz (25 g) sultanas
1 oz (25 g) Rice Krispies
4 oz (110 g) plain cooking
  chocolate

Gently melt the margarine and sugar in a pan and stir in the dates, cherries and sultanas. Add the Rice Krispies to form a soft sticky mixture, spread this into a greased Swiss roll tin and allow to cool. Melt the chocolate and pour over the mixture. Cool and set in the refrigerator. Cut into nine squares and lift out of the tin. Cut each square in half diagonally to form triangle shapes.

LEMON AND HONEY SPONGE LAYER SLICES
Makes 12

4 oz (110 g) butter or margarine
2 oz (50 g) soft brown sugar
2 level tbsp honey
grated rind and juice of 1 lemon

2 eggs, beaten
8 oz (225 g) self-raising flour
1 level tsp baking powder

Filling:
4 level tbsp lemon curd

2 oz (50 g) butter or margarine

Icing:
12 oz (350 g) icing sugar
2 tbsp water

12 lemon jelly slices

Preheat the oven to 375°F/190°C/Gas Mk 5. Melt the margarine or butter in a small pan and stir in the sugar and honey. Add all but one teaspoon of the lemon juice and rind to the pan, stir, then transfer to a bowl. When cold beat in the eggs, and sift in the flour and baking powder. Pour into a base lined and greased Swiss roll tin and bake above the centre of the oven for 25-30 minutes. Cool in the tin for about 5 minutes, then turn out onto a wire rack and cut in half when cold. Meanwhile beat the lemon curd with the butter or margarine for the filling and sandwich the cake together. Sift the icing sugar into a bowl, then add the water and reserved lemon juice. Spread the icing over the top and sides of the cake and decorate with the 12 lemon jelly slices. Cut when the icing has set.

CORNFLAKE CRUNCHIES
Makes 12

6 oz (175 g) margarine
3 oz (75 g) caster sugar
4 oz (110 g) desiccated coconut
6 oz (175 g) self-raising flour, sifted
2 oz (50 g) cornflakes
grated rind of 1 lemon

Preheat the oven to 350°F/180°C/Gas Mk 4. Melt the margarine and sugar in a pan over a low heat, then set aside to cool. Mix together with the flour and coconut, then gently fold in the cornflakes and lemon rind. Place the mixture in a greased Swiss roll tin. Cook in the centre of the oven for 30-35 minutes until a light golden in colour. Cool in the tin, but make into 12 fingers with a sharp knife whilst still warm.

RASPBERRY ROUNDS
Makes 15

8 oz (225 g) plain flour
2 tsp baking powder
3 oz (75 g) butter or hard
  margarine, cut
  into pieces

4 oz (110 g) caster sugar
pinch of salt
3 oz (75 g) raspberry jam
6 tbsp milk
caster sugar, for sprinkling

Preheat the oven to 375°F/190°C/Gas Mk 5. Sift the flour, baking powder and salt into a bowl. Rub in the butter or margarine until mixture resembles fine breadcrumbs. Stir in the sugar, add the milk and mix to a firm dough. Knead the dough on a lightly floured surface until smooth. Roll out into fifteen circles 4 inches (10 cm) in diameter. Place a teaspoonful of jam in the centre of each circle. Moisten the edges of the dough lightly and pull together to the centre on top to enclose the jam. Lightly grease and flour two baking sheets. Arrange the cakes on the baking sheets and cut a small cross on the top of each. Bake in oven for 15 minutes. Sprinkle with caster sugar and bake for a further 5 minutes. Cool on a wire rack.

DATE CRUNCHIES
Makes 36

8 oz (225 g) block of dates, chopped into squares
1 tbsp clear honey
1 level tbsp lemon juice
4 tbsp water
¼ level tsp mixed spice ·
6 oz (175 g) butter
6 oz (175 g) self-raising flour, sifted
6 oz (175 g) semolina
3 oz (75 g) caster sugar

Preheat the oven to 400°F/200°C/Gas Mk 6. Put the dates in a saucepan with the lemon juice, honey, water and mixed spice. Cover and simmer very gently over a low heat until soft. Stir frequently, so that the mixture does not stick and burn. Remove from the heat and beat to a smooth consistency. Leave to cool. Melt the butter in a large pan. Remove from the heat and stir in the sugar, flour and semolina. Spoon half of this mixture over the base of a greased Swiss roll tin. Press evenly over the tin, then cover with the date mixture. Crumble the rest of the flour and semolina mixture in a layer over the top. Bake for 30 minutes until golden brown. Leave for 10 minutes before cutting into fingers and removing carefully from the tin.

GINGER WHIRLS
Makes 12

8 oz (225 g) butter
3 oz (75 g) icing sugar
7 oz (200 g) plain flour

1 oz (25 g) cornflour
2 tsp ground ginger
2 tbsp ginger marmalade

Preheat the oven to 375°F/190°C/Gas Mk 5. Cream the butter and icing sugar in a bowl until light and fluffy. Fold in the sifted flour, cornflour and ground ginger. Place the mixture into a piping bag fitted with a large star nozzle. Arrange 12 paper cake cases on a baking tray, and pipe in the mixture using a spiral motion. Bake in oven for 15-20 minutes until golden brown. Transfer to a wire rack to cool. Place a little ginger marmalade in the centre of each whirl.

QUEEN CAKES
Makes 16

4 oz (110 g) butter
4 oz (110 g) caster sugar
2 eggs, beaten
4 oz (110 g) self-raising flour, sifted
2 oz (50 g) sultanas

Preheat the oven to 375°F/190°C/Gas Mk 5. In a bowl, cream together the butter and sugar until fluffy. Beat in the egg, a little at a time. Fold in the flour and then stir in the fruit. Arrange sixteen paper cake cases on baking sheets and spoon the mixture into them. Bake in oven for 15-20 minutes until golden. Transfer to a wire rack to cool.

FLAPJACKS
Makes 16

4 oz (110 g) margarine
4 oz (110 g) soft brown sugar

8 oz (225 g) rolled oats
2 level tbsp golden syrup

Grease an 8 inch (20 cm) square tin and preheat the oven to 350°F/180°C/Gas Mk 4. Melt the margarine, sugar and syrup in a pan. Mix in the rolled oats, pack the mixture into the tin and bake for 20-25 minutes. Allow to cool slightly, then mark into slices. Remove from the tin onto a wire tray when almost cold.

GINGER FLAPJACKS
Makes 16

4 oz (110 g) margarine
2 level tbsp golden syrup
8 oz (225 g) rolled oats
1 level tsp ground ginger
4 oz (110 g) soft brown sugar

Topping:
6 level tbsp icing sugar, sifted
3 oz (75 g) butter
1 level tsp ground ginger
3 level tsp golden syrup

Preheat the oven to 350°F/180°C/Gas Mk 4. Grease an 8 inch (20 cm) square tin. Melt the margarine and syrup in a pan, mix in the rolled oats, ginger and sugar and pack the mixture into the tin. Bake for 20-25 minutes. To make the topping, gently melt all the ingredients over a low heat. Pour on top of the flapjacks and leave to set. Cut into squares when cold.

CINNAMON CHERRY BARS

4 oz (110 g) ground almonds
1 egg, beaten
8 oz (225 g) plain flour
8 oz (225 g) caster sugar
6 oz (175 g) butter

1 tsp ground cinnamon
finely grated rind of 1 lemon
4 oz (110 g) black cherry jam
icing sugar

Put the almonds, egg, flour, sugar, butter, cinnamon and lemon rind in a large bowl. Beat well together, then knead lightly. Cover the bowl and place in refrigerator for 30 minutes. Divide the dough in half and firmly press one half evenly into a lightly greased 11 x 7 inch (28 x 18 cm) shallow baking tin. Spread over the black cherry jam. Roll out the remaining dough on a lightly floured surface and cut into pencil thin strips. Arrange these over the jam to form a lattice pattern. Chill in the refrigerator for 30 minutes. Preheat the oven to 350°F/180°C/Gas Mk 4. Bake for 40 minutes until golden and firm. Leave to cool in the tin and then sprinkle with icing sugar. Cut into 24 bars and remove and store in box.

CHERRY MARSHMALLOW BARS
Makes 12 slices

Base:
4 oz (110 g) butter or soft margarine
2 tbsp cocoa powder
4 oz (110 g) icing sugar
3½ oz (90 g) desiccated coconut

6 oz (175 g) digestive biscuits, crushed
½ tsp vanilla essence
1 egg, beaten

Topping:
1 lb (450 g) caster sugar
1 level tbsp gelatine
6 tbsp cold water
5 tbsp boiling water

glacé cherries and flaked
* almonds, as desired*
plain chocolate

Melt the butter gently in a large saucepan and add the cocoa powder, icing sugar and coconut and stir well. When mixed add the crushed digestive biscuits, the vanilla essence and the beaten egg. Cook very gently for a few minutes, stirring, and then turn out into a greased and lined 10 inch (25 cm) loose-bottomed baking tin or deep flan ring and leave to set. For the topping, put the gelatine into a small bowl, add 1 tablespoon cold water and leave to dissolve. Add the boiling water. Chop up the glacé cherries and mix with flaked almonds. Put the caster sugar in a mixer and add the remaining 5 tablespoons cold water. Whisk for 5 minutes. Add the dissolved gelatine and continue to whisk until the mixture becomes meringue-like. Fold in the cherries and almonds and pour on top of the base. Melt the chocolate in a bowl over simmering water and then dribble on top of the meringue mixture. Leave to set before cutting into bars.

SWISS TARTS
Makes 12

8 oz (225 g) butter
2 oz (50 g) caster sugar
vanilla essence

8 oz (225 g) plain flour
icing sugar
2 tbsp redcurrant jelly

Preheat the oven to 350°F/180°C/Gas Mk 4. In a bowl, cream together the butter and sugar then stir in a few drops of vanilla essence and gradually stir in the flour. Place the mixture in a piping bag fitted with a large star nozzle and pipe into 12 paper cake cases on a baking sheet using a spiral motion. Leave a small hollow in the centre of each. Bake in the oven for 25-30 minutes until golden brown. Leave to cool, then sprinkle icing sugar on top. Place a little redcurrant jelly in the hollow in the centre of each cake.

GINGER-FLAVOURED CHEESE BARS
Makes 10

2 oz (50 g) soft margarine
6 oz (175 g) ginger nut biscuits, crushed

Filling:
8 oz (225 g) curd cheese
2 oz (50 g) caster sugar
2 level tbsp lemon curd
1 oz (25 g) cornflour, sifted
1 large egg, beaten
crystallised ginger pieces

Preheat the oven to 375°F/190°C/Gas Mk 5. Melt the margarine in a large saucepan and stir in the crushed biscuits. The easiest way to do this is to put them in a plastic bag and crush with a rolling pin. Press the biscuit mix into a greased and base lined 7 inch (18 cm) square cake tin. Beat the cheese and sugar together until smooth, then beat in the lemon curd and cornflour. Then add the beaten egg and beat again. Pour over the biscuit mix and bake in the centre of the oven for 25 minutes or until the topping is firm. Slip a knife round the edges of the tray bake but leave in the tin to cool. Decorate with small pieces of crystallised ginger.

BANANA ROCK CAKES
Makes about 10

7 oz (200 g) plain wholemeal flour
1½ tsp baking powder
3 oz (75 g) butter
1 tbsp light brown soft sugar
2 oz (50 g) sultanas
8 oz (225 g) bananas
1 tsp lemon juice
1 egg

Preheat the oven to 400°F/200°C/Gas Mk 6. Sift the flour and baking powder into a bowl. Rub in the butter until the mixture resembles fine breadcrumbs. Stir in the sugar and sultanas. Mash the bananas in a bowl then add the lemon juice. Beat in the egg. Pour into the flour mixture and beat well. Place about ten spoonfuls of the mixture on a baking sheet, arranged to leave room for spreading. Bake in oven for 15 minutes until risen and golden brown. Cool on a wire rack.

FUDGE BROWNIES
Makes 15

*4 oz (110 g) butter or soft
  margarine
8 oz (225 g) soft brown sugar
2 eggs
1 tsp vanilla essence*

*2 oz (50 g) plain flour
1 oz (25 g) cocoa powder
¼ level tsp baking powder
4 oz (110 g) chopped walnuts
1 tbsp milk*

*Topping:
3 oz (75 g) plain chocolate
1 oz (25 g) butter
1 tbsp boiling water*

*2 tbsp milk
1 tsp coffee
6 oz (175 g) icing sugar*

Preheat the oven to 350°F/180°C/Gas Mk 4. Cream the butter and sugar together until light and fluffy in colour and texture. Beat in the eggs one at a time, adding a little flour to bind if the mixture starts to curdle. Stir in the vanilla essence. Sift the flour, cocoa powder and baking powder together and fold into the creamed mixture with a metal spoon, alternately with the walnuts and milk. Grease and base line a Swiss roll tin and pour the mixture in, levelling the top. Bake in the centre of the oven for about 35 minutes or until the cake is firm to the touch. Turn out, remove base lining and leave to cool on a wire rack. For the topping, melt the chocolate in a bowl over a saucepan of hot water, add the milk, butter and the coffee dissolved in a little water. Stir in the sifted icing sugar and beat until smooth. Spread over the cake, leave to set and then cut into squares.

COCONUT KISSES
Makes 10

*3 oz (75 g) margarine
2 oz (50 g) sugar
4 oz (110 g) self-raising flour, sifted*

*a little milk
jam
desiccated coconut*

Preheat the oven to 400°F/200°C/Gas Mk 6. In a bowl, cream together the margarine and sugar. Add the flour and sufficient milk to make a firm dough. Form the dough into small marble-sized balls and arrange on an ungreased baking sheet. Bake in oven for 10 minutes. Cool on the baking sheet. When completely cold, sandwich together two by two using the jam. Brush all over with more jam and roll in the desiccated coconut.

BETTY'S BROWNIES
Makes 16-20

6 oz *(175 g) butter, melted*
6 oz *(175 g) caster sugar*
1 tsp *vanilla essence*
¼ tsp *salt*
3 *eggs*

2 oz *(50 g) unsweetened cocoa*
    powder
½ tsp *baking powder*
6 oz *(175 g) plain flour*
2 oz *(50 g) chopped nuts*

Preheat the oven to 350°F/180°C/Gas Mk 4. Butter an 8 inch (20 cm) square shallow cake tin. Mix together the melted butter and sugar, beating well. Add the vanilla essence, salt and eggs and beat well again. Sift the cocoa powder, baking powder and flour together and add to the mixture, mixing until smooth. Stir in the chopped nuts, pour into the tin and bake in a preheated oven for 25-30 minutes or until firm to the touch. Cool in the tin before cutting with a sharp knife. The brownies can be covered with chocolate icing before cutting if desired.

ORANGE MERINGUE BARS
Makes 12-14

4 oz *(110 g) butter*
4 oz *(110 g) caster sugar*
3 *eggs, separated*
grated rind of 1 orange
2 tbsp *orange juice*
8 oz *(225 g) self-raising flour*
2 oz *(50 g) walnuts, chopped*
6 oz *(175 g) sifted icing sugar*

Preheat the oven to 325°F/170°C/Gas Mk 3. Cream the butter and sugar in a bowl until light and fluffy. Beat in the egg yolks, followed by the orange rind and juice. Add the flour and beat until fairly stiff. Line a Swiss roll tin with non-stick parchment paper and press in the dough spreading evenly over the tin. Sprinkle on the walnuts. Place the egg whites in a bowl and whisk until very stiff. Whisk in half the amount of icing sugar a little at a time and then carefully fold in the remaining sugar retaining 1 tbsp. Spread the mixture evenly on top of the almonds, using a fork to form it into peaks. Sprinkle over the 1 tbsp of icing sugar and bake for 45 minutes until a light brown colour. Remove from the oven and allow to cool then cut into bars.

ECCLES CAKES

1 lb (450 g) shortcrust pastry
4 oz (110 g) currants
1 oz (25 g) chopped mixed peel
½ tsp ground allspice
½ tsp ground nutmeg

2 oz (50 g) dark brown sugar
1 oz (25 g) butter
1 egg white
½ oz (10 g) caster sugar

Preheat the oven to 425°F/220°C/Gas Mk 7. Roll out the pastry and cut into 4 inch (10 cm) circles. Mix together the currants, chopped peel and spices. Melt the dark brown sugar and butter together and stir into the fruit mixture. Cool completely. Put a spoonful into the centre of each pastry circle. Pull the edges of the pastry together over the filling and seal them firmly by pinching together. Turn them over and press lightly to flatten. Put them on a baking sheet and make a small hole in the centre of each. Brush with egg white and sprinkle with caster sugar. Bake in the oven for 15 minutes. Transfer to a wire rack to cool.

CRUMBLY CHOCOLATE SQUARES
Makes 15

7 oz (200 g) butter
4 level tbsp drinking chocolate
* powder*
2 level tbsp golden syrup
grated rind of 1 lemon

14 oz (400 g) packet digestive
* biscuits*
2 chocolate Aero bars
* (flavoured if preferred)*

Heat the butter, chocolate powder, syrup and finely grated lemon rind in a large saucepan until melted and stir well. Break the biscuits by placing them in a bag and crushing with a rolling pin, then stir into the melted mixture. Spoon the mixture into a lightly greased small Swiss roll tin, pressing down well. Set in the refrigerator for 1 hour. Melt the chocolate bars and spread over the biscuit cake. Leave to set before cutting into squares.

WALNUT KISSES
Makes 10

3 oz (75 g) margarine
2 oz (50 g) sugar
4 oz (110 g) self-raising flour,
* sifted*

a little milk
jam
walnuts, finely chopped

Preheat the oven to 400°F/200°C/Gas Mk 6. In a bowl, cream together the margarine and sugar. Add the flour and sufficient milk to make a firm dough. Form the dough into small, marble-sized balls and arrange on an ungreased baking sheet. Bake for 10 minutes. Cool on the sheet. When completely cold, use the jam to sandwich together two by two. Brush all over with more jam and roll in the walnuts.

EXOTIC FRUIT ROCK CAKES
Makes 12

12 oz (350 g) plain flour	3 oz (75 g) dried pineapple pieces
3 tsp baking powder	3 oz (75 g) dried papaya pieces
1 tsp mixed spice	3 oz (75 g) demerara sugar
6 oz (175 g) butter	2 eggs, size 3, beaten
2 oz (50 g) desiccated coconut	3 tbsp milk

Preheat the oven to 400°F/200°C/Gas Mk 6. Lightly grease two baking sheets. Sift the flour, baking powder and mixed spice into a large mixing bowl and rub in the butter until the mixture resembles fine breadcrumbs. Stir in the coconut, dried pineapple, dried papaya and sugar and make a well in the centre. Beat the eggs and milk together and pour into the centre of the mix, binding lightly with a fork until a stiff, crumbly mixture is obtained. Place six rough heaps of the mixture on each of the greased baking sheets and bake for about 20 minutes in a preheated oven, or until golden brown. Cool on a wire rack.

CHOCOLATE MERINGUES

2 egg whites
pinch of salt
pinch of cream of tartar
6 oz (175 g) caster sugar
6 oz (175 g) plain chocolate

Preheat the oven to 300°F/150°C/Gas Mk 2. Whisk the egg whites with the salt and cream of tartar until they form soft peaks. Add the sugar gradually, beating until the mixture is stiff and shiny. Break the chocolate into small pieces and stir into the mixture. Cover baking sheets with greaseproof paper and drop on rounded teaspoonfuls of the mixture. Bake in the oven for 30 minutes. Turn the meringues over and cook for another 10 minutes. Cool on a wire rack. Do not fill these meringues with cream.

DANISH LOVE RINGS

9 oz (250 g) self-raising flour, sifted
4½ oz (125 g) caster sugar
grated rind of 1 orange
pinch of salt
3 hard-boiled egg yolks
9 oz (250 g) lightly salted butter, softened

Mix the flour, sugar, grated orange rind and salt together. Sieve the egg yolks and add them. Finally cut the softened butter in small pieces into the bowl and mix to a smooth dough with as little kneading as possible, wrap in clingfilm and chill for 1 hour. Preheat the oven to 425°F/220°C/Gas Mk 7. Break off pieces and, using your hands, roll them on a board to 3½ inches (8.5 cm) lengths of pencil thickness. Join the two ends to form into rings. Place on baking sheets lined with non-stick parchment, leaving room for them to expand a little, and bake for 8 minutes or more until they are lightly golden. Leave on a wire tray to cool. Eat plain or they can be coated with orange glacé icing if liked.

SCONES

WHOLEMEAL FRUIT SCONES
Makes 18

8 oz (225 g) plain wholemeal flour
1 tbsp baking powder
1 tsp mixed spice
4 oz (110 g) butter or margarine
1 oz (25 g) light soft brown sugar
4 oz (110 g) mixed dried fruit
¼ pt (150 ml) milk

Preheat the oven to 425°F/220°C/Gas Mk 7. Sift the flour, baking powder and spice together in a bowl. Rub in the fat until the mixture resembles fine breadcrumbs. Stir in the sugar and fruit. Add egg and sufficient milk to mix to a soft dough. Knead lightly on a floured board and roll out to ¼ inch (2 cm) thick. Cut into rounds 1½-2 inches (4-5 cm) across and place close together on a greased baking sheet. Bake for 15 minutes and then cool on a wire rack.

PIKELETS
Makes 12

8 oz (225 g) plain flour, sifted
pinch of salt
2 oz (50 g) caster sugar

¼ pt (150 ml) milk
1 tsp bicarbonate of soda
2 tbsp boiling water

Sift the flour and salt into a bowl and stir in the sugar. Beat in the milk. Dissolve the bicarbonate of soda in the boiling water then beat into the batter. Drop tablespoons of the batter onto a hot griddle or heavy frying pan. Cook on both sides until golden brown all over. These are best eaten hot with butter.

COTTAGE CHEESE DROP SCONES
Makes 10

4 oz (110 g) cottage cheese
1 tbsp melted butter
2 oz (50 g) self-raising flour, sifted

2 eggs, beaten
1 tbsp milk

Mix the cottage cheese and butter together in a large bowl, then gradually work in the flour, eggs and milk to make a smooth, thick batter. Drop tablespoons of the batter onto a greased, heavy frying pan or griddle and cook over moderate heat until the surface of the mixture bubbles. Turn over and cook other side until golden brown. Serve immediately, spread with honey or jam.

SWEET DROP SCONES
Makes 12

8 oz (225 g) plain flour, sifted
1 tsp cream of tartar
½ tsp bicarbonate of soda
½ tsp salt

1 oz (25 g) caster sugar
1 egg, beaten
8 fl oz (250 ml) milk
1 tbsp oil

Sift the flour, cream of tartar, bicarbonate of soda and salt into a bowl, then stir in the sugar. Gradually beat in the egg, milk and oil to make a thick, creamy batter. Lightly grease a heavy frying pan and drop in tablespoons of the batter. Cook over moderate heat until the surface bubbles. Turn over and continue to cook until golden on the underside. Wrap the warm scones in a clean tea towel until all the mixture is cooked.

CINNAMON DROP SCONES
Makes 24

8 oz (225 g) self-raising flour
1 tsp ground cinnamon
½ tsp bicarbonate of soda
1 tsp cream of tartar

2 tbsp caster sugar
1 egg
½ pint (300 ml) milk
4 tbsp oil

Sift the flour, cinnamon, bicarbonate of soda and cream of tartar into a bowl. Stir in the sugar. Add the egg and a little milk and whisk until smooth. Gradually whisk in the remaining milk and mix well. Heat the oil in a large, heavy-based frying pan, swirl the oil around the pan and pour off the excess. Drop tablespoonfuls of the mixture into the pan, spaced well apart, and cook for 1-2 minutes until bubbles appear on the surface and the underside is golden. Turn the scones over and cook until golden. Remove from the pan and keep warm, loosely wrapped in a tea towel. Repeat with the remaining mixture, oiling the pan between batches. Serve hot, spead with butter and honey or maple syrup.

WELSH CAKES
Makes 16

8 oz (225 g) plain flour
½ tsp baking powder
¼ tsp salt
¼ tsp mixed spice
2 oz (50 g) margarine

2 oz (50 g) lard
3 oz (75 g) caster sugar
2 oz (50 g) currants
1 egg, beaten
milk to mix

For this recipe you will need a heavy-based fying pan or a griddle. Lightly flour the pan or griddle and place over a low heat. Sieve the flour, baking powder, salt and mixed spice into a bowl. Add the margarine and lard, cut into small pieces and rub in until the mixture resembles fine breadcrumbs. Stir in the caster sugar and the currants. Place the beaten egg in a measuring jug and add the milk until the combined liquids measure 4 fl oz (100 ml). Beat lightly with a fork and then stir into the flour mixture with a knife until a soft but workable dough is formed. Roll the dough out on a lightly floured board to ¼ inch (0.5 cm) thickness and cut into 2 inch (5 cm) rounds with a plain cutter. Wipe off any excess flour from the pan or griddle and cook the rounds for about 4 minutes on each side until golden brown. Serve hot with butter.

CHEESE SCONES
Makes 15

8 oz (225 g) self-raising flour, sifted
1 tsp mustard powder
½ tsp salt
pinch of paprika pepper

2 oz (50 g) butter
4 oz (110 g) Cheddar cheese, grated
1 egg, beaten

Glaze: 2 tbsp milk or beaten egg and milk

Preheat oven to 400°F/200°C/Gas Mk 6. Sift the flour, mustard powder, salt and pepper into a bowl. Rub in the butter until the mixture resembles fine breadcrumbs. Stir in 3 oz (75 g) of the cheese. Beat in the egg and sufficient milk to mix to a soft dough. Knead very lightly, place on a floured surface and roll out to ¾ inch (2 cm) thick. Cut into rounds 1½-2 inches (4-5 cm) in diameter and place close together on a greased baking sheet. Brush with beaten egg or milk and sprinkle with the remaining cheese. Bake in the oven for 20 minutes and cool on a wire rack.

BARLEY BANNOCKS
Makes 8

1 lb (450 g) barley meal
4 oz (110 g) plain flour
2 tsp cream of tartar

½ tsp salt
2 tsp bicarbonate of soda
12 fl oz (350 ml) buttermilk

Mix the barley meal, flour, cream of tartar and salt in a bowl. Stir the bicarbonate of soda into the milk and pour into the flour. Work to a soft dough and roll out on a floured surface to ½ inch (1 cm) thick. Cut into rounds about the size of a small plate. Cook in a greased thick frying pan until golden brown. Turn over and cook until the underside is golden. Serve fresh.

HOT APPLE SCONES
Makes 8-10

3 large cooking apples, peeled,
  cored and finely chopped
8 oz (225 g) flour, sifted
1 tsp baking powder

3 oz (75 g) lard
2 oz (50 g) soft brown sugar
1 egg, beaten
a little butter

Topping: caster sugar

Prepare the apples. Preheat the oven to 350°F/180°C/Gas Mk 4. Sift the baking powder and flour together with a pinch of salt. Rub in the lard. Stir in the sugar. Add the egg to the mixture with the finely chopped apples. Work the mixture together, adding a little milk if it is too dry, but make sure it is not too wet as the apples will moisten the scones when baking. Put into a greased shallow Swiss roll tin. Bake for 30 minutes or until golden and cooked. Tip out and cut into rounds with a scone cutter. Split open and butter, and then dust with caster sugar before serving.

DROP SCONES
Makes 20-24

8 oz (225 g) self-raising flour
pinch of salt
2 oz (50 g) caster sugar

2 eggs, beaten,
½ pt (300 ml) milk

Sift the flour and salt together and stir in the beaten eggs, adding enough milk to give a thick batter. Beat until smooth. Heat a griddle or a heavy-based frying pan, sprinkle on a little flour and cook gently until the flour goes brown. This should take 1½-2 minutes if the pan is at the correct temperature. Wipe off the flour and rub with a little lard. Put tablespoons of batter in the pan, spacing out to allow the scones to spread a little. Cook until bubbles form on the surface of the scones, then turn over with a spatula or flat bladed knife and cook until the underside is golden brown. (About 2-3 minutes each side.) Place on greaseproof paper on a cooling rack and cover with a clean tea towel. Continue until all the batter has been used up.
Serve warm, spread with butter.

PLAIN BUNS
Makes 15-18

8 oz (225 g) self-raising flour, sifted   *2 oz (50 g) butter or margarine*
1 tsp baking powder   *1 egg , beaten*
pinch of salt   *8 fl oz (250 ml) milk*

Preheat the oven to 425°F/220°C/Gas Mk 7. Sift the flour, baking powder and salt into a bowl. Rub in the fat until the mixture resembles fine breadcrumbs. Add the egg and milk and beat well. Spoon the mixture into 15-18 greased deep patty tins and bake for 15 minutes. Cool on a wire rack. These can be served split and buttered, either warm or cold.

AMERICAN MUFFINS
Makes 12

8 oz (225 g) plain flour, sifted   *1 egg, beaten*
2½ tsp baking powder   *2 oz (50 g) butter, melted*
2 tbsp caster sugar   *7 fl oz (200 ml) milk*
½ tsp salt

Preheat the oven to 400°F/200°C/Gas Mk 6. Sift dry ingredients into a bowl and add the beaten egg, melted butter and milk. Beat well until smooth. Pour into well-greased deep bun tins. Bake for 25 minutes until well risen and golden in colour. Serve with butter and jam.

TREACLE DROP SCONES
Makes 12-15

8 oz (225 g) self-raising flour,   *1 egg , beaten*
* sifted*   *2 tbsp black treacle*
½ tsp salt   *½ pt (300 ml) milk*
½ tsp ground nutmeg   *3 oz (75 g) seedless raisins*
2 tsp caster sugar

Sift the flour, salt and nutmeg into a bowl and stir in the sugar. Beat together the egg, treacle and milk in another bowl, then mix into the flour to give a creamy batter. Grease and heat a heavy frying pan or griddle and drop tablespoons of the mixture onto it. Place five or six raisins on top of each one. When the batter is set and the scones have risen, turn over and cook undersides until golden. Wrap the warm scones in a clean tea towel as they cool to keep them soft. Serve fresh.

POTATO SCONES
Makes 12

8 oz (225 g) peeled potatoes
2 oz (50 g) butter
4 oz (110 g) plain flour

½ tsp baking powder
¼ tsp salt

Boil the potatoes in lightly salted water until tender. Drain well and mash with the butter. Preheat the oven to 425°F/220°C/Gas Mk 7. Sift the flour, baking powder and salt into a bowl, then add the potatoes and mix well. Knead to make a soft firm dough. Roll out the dough on a floured surface to a thickness of ½ inch (1 cm). Cut into 3 inch (7.5 cm) rounds with a plain cutter and prick once or twice with a fork. Place on lightly floured baking sheet and cook in the oven for 10 minutes. Serve hot with butter.

IRISH BANNOCK
Makes 6-8 wedges

12 oz (350 g) plain flour
1 tsp bicarbonate of soda
1 tsp cream of tartar
1 oz (25 g) caster sugar

4 oz (110 g) sultanas
½ pt (300 ml) buttermilk
or sour milk
caster sugar for dredging

Preheat the oven to 400°F/200°C/Gas Mk 6. Sift the flour, bicarbonate of soda and cream of tartar into a bowl, then stir in the sugar and sultanas. Add the milk and mix well to form a soft dough. Spread the dough into a well-greased 7 inch (18 cm) sandwich tin and bake in oven for 30 minutes. Remove from tin and sprinkle caster sugar over the top. Wrap the bannock in a clean tea cloth and leave on a wire rack to cool. Serve sliced with butter.

YOGHURT DROP SCONES
Makes 8

3 oz (75 g) self-raising flour, sifted
pinch of salt

¼ pt (150 ml) natural yoghurt
1 egg

Sift the flour and salt into a bowl. Mix in the yoghurt and egg to make a thick creamy batter. Drop tablespoons of the batter onto a greased thick frying pan and cook over moderate heat until the surface bubbles. Turn over and cook until the undersides are golden. Wrap in a clean tea towel to keep scones soft as they cool.

BRAN SCONES
Makes 18

12 oz (350 g) plain wholemeal flour   *3 oz (75 g) butter or margarine*
3 oz (75 g) bran   *3 oz (75 g) light soft brown sugar*
1 tbsp baking powder   *1 beaten egg*
pinch of salt   *½ pt (300 ml) milk*

Preheat the oven to 425°F/220°C/Gas Mk 7. Mix the flour, bran, baking powder and salt together in a bowl. Rub in the fat until the mixture resembles fine breadcrumbs. Stir in the sugar. Add the egg and sufficient milk to mix to a soft dough. Lightly knead, then place on a floured surface and roll out to ¾ inch (2 cm) thick. Cut into rounds 1-2 inches (2.5-5 cm) in diameter and place on a greased baking sheet. Bake for 15 minutes and cool on a wire rack.

BACON AND SEED SCONES
Makes 8

8 oz (225 g) wholemeal flour   *4 rashers bacon, fried and chopped*
pinch of salt   *5 fl oz (150 ml) natural yoghurt*
2 oz (50 g) soft margarine   *1 tsp bicarbonate of soda*
4 tbsp sunflower seeds

Preheat the oven to 425°F/220°C/Gas Mk 7. In a bowl, stir together the flour and salt, add the margarine and rub in until mixture resembles breadcrumbs. Stir in the bacon and sunflower seeds. Place the yoghurt and bicarbonate of soda in a small bowl, mix together and leave for about 2 minutes until frothy. Add this mixture to the flour and knead well to a soft dough. Place on floured surface and roll out to a thickness of about ½ inch (1 cm). Cut out rounds about 2 inches (5 cm) in diameter and place on a greased baking sheet. Bake in oven for 10 minutes until risen. Remove to a wire rack to cool.

RAISIN AND PEANUT SCONES
Makes 8

8 oz (225 g) wholemeal flour
pinch of salt
2 oz (50 g) soft margarine
1 oz (25 g) raisins

1 oz (25 g) unsalted peanuts
1 tbsp clear honey
5 fl oz (150 ml) natural yoghurt
1 tsp bicarbonate of soda

Preheat the oven to 425°F/220°C/Gas Mk 7. In a bowl, sift together the flour and salt, add the margarine and rub in until mixture resembles breadcrumbs. Stir in the raisins and peanuts and add the honey. Place the yoghurt and bicarbonate of soda in a small bowl, mix together and leave for about 2 minutes until frothy. Add this mixture to the flour and knead well to a soft dough. Place on a floured surface and roll out to a thickness of about ½ inch (1 cm). Cut out rounds of about 2 inches (5 cm) and place on a greased baking sheet. Bake in oven for 10 minutes until risen. Remove to a wire rack to cool.

WHOLEMEAL SCONES
Makes 8

8 oz (225 g) wholemeal flour
pinch of salt
2 oz (50 g) soft margarine

5 fl oz (150 ml) natural yoghurt
1 tsp bicarbonate of soda

Preheat the oven to 425°F/220°C/Gas Mk 7. In a bowl, sift together the flour and salt, add the margarine and rub in until mixture resembles breadcrumbs. Place the yoghurt and bicarbonate of soda in a small bowl, mix together and leave for about 2 minutes until frothy. Add this mixture to the flour and knead well to a soft dough. Turn out on a floured surface and roll out to a thickness of about ½ inch (1 cm). Cut out rounds about 2 inches (5 cm) in diameter and place on a greased baking sheet. Bake for 10 minutes until risen. Remove to a wire rack to cool.

PASTRIES

LEMON CUSTARD TARTS
Makes 8

4 oz (110 g) plain flour, sifted
2 oz (50 g) margarine, cut into small pieces
2 oz (50 g) caster sugar
1 egg, beaten

Filling:
3 oz (75 g) caster sugar
1 tbsp custard powder
grated rind and juice of 1 lemon
½ pt (300 ml) water
¼ pt (150 ml) whipping cream to decorate

Sift the flour into a bowl and add the margarine. Rub into the flour until the mixture resembles fine breadcrumbs. Stir in the caster sugar and sufficient beaten egg (about half) to bind the pastry together into a soft, pliable dough. Wrap in clingfilm and refrigerate for 1½ hours until firm. Roll the pastry out on a floured board to about ¼ inch (5 mm) thickness. Cut into rounds with a fluted 3 inch (7.5 cm) cutter and use it to line lightly oiled patty tins. Chill while making the filling. Preheat the oven to 400°F/200°C/Gas Mk 6. To make the filling, put the sugar, custard powder, lemon rind and juice into a small saucepan. Blend in enough water to make a smooth paste, then stir in the rest of the water. Bring gently to the boil, stirring, until the custard becomes thick and opaque. Remove from the heat, leave to cool for a couple of minutes, stirring from time to time to prevent a skin forming, and then stir in the rest of the beaten egg. Fill the chilled pastry rounds three-quarters full then bake towards the top of the oven for 12-15 minutes or until the pastry is cooked. Allow to cool in the tins. Whisk the cream until thick and pipe a rosette on top of each tartlet when they are cold. These are best made the same day you are going to serve them otherwise the pastry may become soggy.

STICKY NUT PIE
Makes 8 portions

6 oz (175 g)) plain flour, sifted
pinch of salt
6 oz (175 g) butter
1 tbsp sugar
3 eggs and 1 yolk

8 oz (225 g) soft brown sugar
1 tsp vanilla essence
6 tbsp golden syrup
8 oz (225 g) mixed nuts,
roughly chopped

Sift flour and pinch of salt into a bowl. Rub in half the butter until mixture resembles fine crumbs. Stir in sugar and egg yolk with enough cold water to form a soft dough. Knead the pastry lightly and roll out thinly on a lightly floured surface to a circle about 11 inches (28 cm) in diameter. Lift the pastry over a rolling pin and lay over a 9 inch (23 cm) loose-bottomed flan tin. Press pastry into sides of flan tin. Level top with a rolling pin. Chill pastry case for 30 minutes. Preheat the oven to 425°F/220°C/Gas Mk 7. Line pastry case with paper and baking beans (for baking blind) and cook for 10 minutes, then remove beans and paper and cook for a further 5 minutes. Reduce the heat to 350°F/180°C/Gas Mk 4. In a large bowl, whisk together the eggs, sugar and vanilla until very thick. Melt remaining butter and syrup in a saucepan, then stir into the egg mixture with half the chopped nuts. Pour the nut mixture into the pastry case and sprinkle with nuts. Cook for 35 minutes until golden and set. Serve warm with whipped cream.

PALMIERS
Makes 32

8 oz (225 g) packet frozen puff pastry, thawed
a little water
2 oz (50 g) demerara sugar
2 tsp ground cinnamon

Preheat the oven to 425°F/220°C/Gas Mk 7. Roll out the pastry and trim to a rectangle 12 x 10 inches (30 x 25 cm) and cut into 2 rectangles 6 x 10 inches (15 x 25 cm). For each rectangle: brush lightly with water, sprinkle with a quarter of the sugar and spice. Fold the long sides to meet in the centre. Flatten a little. Brush lightly with water and sprinkle with another quarter of sugar and spice. Fold pastry in half lengthways, pressing down lightly. Cut each length into 16 slices. Put slices, cut-side down, on to wetted baking sheet and flatten a little with a palette knife. Bake for 10 minutes. Turn palmiers over, return to oven for 3 minutes. Cool on wire tray.

WALNUT TART
Makes 8 slices

Pastry:
8 oz (225 g) plain flour, sifted
2 tbsp icing sugar
4 oz (110 g) butter or soft margarine

1 large egg, beaten
1 tbsp water

Filling:
4 oz (110 g) butter
4 oz (110 g) soft brown sugar
3 eggs, beaten
5 oz (150 g) golden syrup

8 oz (225 g) walnuts, roughly chopped
juice and grated rind of 1 lemon
pinch of salt

Rub the margarine or butter into the flour and sugar until it resembles fine breadcrumbs. Stir in the egg and enough cold water to mix to a soft dough. Wrap in clingfilm and chill for 20 minutes. Preheat the oven to 350°F/180°C/Gas Mk 4. Roll out the dough on a lightly floured surface and use it to line a 10 inch (25 cm) flan tin. Prick the pastry base with a fork, and bake blind for 10 minutes until lightly cooked. Meanwhile cream together the butter and sugar for the filling until light and smooth, then gradually beat in the eggs. Warm the syrup until it is runny and beat into the creamed mixture, along with the walnuts, lemon rind and juice and the salt. Pour into the pastry case and bake for 45 minutes until well risen and lightly browned.

MARZIPAN PUFFS
Makes 12

13 oz (375 g) packet frozen
 puff pastry, thawed
8 oz (225 g) block marzipan

3-4 tbsp black cherry jam
1 egg white
caster sugar for sprinkling

Preheat the oven to 400°F/200°C/Gas Mk 6. Roll out the pastry on a lightly floured surface to a 16 x 12 inch (40 x 30 cm) rectangle. Then cut into twelve 4 x 4 inch (10 x 10 cm) squares. Roll out the marzipan to a rectangle 12 x 9 inches (30 x 23 cm) and then cut into twelve 3 x 3 inch (7.5 x 7.5 cm) squares. Place a marzipan square in the centre of each pastry square. Place a rounded teaspoon of jam on each marzipan square. Brush the edges of the pastry with lightly beaten egg white and fold to form a triangle. Seal edges well and make two small cuts in the top. Brush with egg white and sprinkle with sugar. Bake for 20-25 minutes until well risen and golden. Sprinkle with more caster sugar and cool on a wire rack.

APPLE AND MARZIPAN TART
Makes 8 portions

6 oz (175 g) hard margarine
10 oz (275g) plain flour, sifted
2 level tbsp caster sugar

1 egg, beaten
1-2 tbsp water

Filling:
4 oz (110 g) marzipan
4 oz (110 g) soft margarine
2 oz (50 g) caster sugar

4 large cooking apples,
    peeled and grated
2 large eggs, separated

Lightly grease a 10 inch (25 cm) loose-bottomed flan tin. Rub the margarine into the flour until the mixture resembles fine crumbs. Add the sugar. Mix in the egg, and, if necessary, enough water to make a firm dough. Chill for 1 hour. Preheat the oven to 425°F/220°C/ Gas Mk 7. Roll out the pastry and use to line the flan tin. Keep pastry trimmings for top. To fill, grate the marzipan over the pastry base. Cream the margarine with the sugar until light and fluffy, then stir in the grated apples. Stiffly whisk the egg whites and fold in with a metal spoon. Spread the apple mixture over the marzipan. Cover with pastry strips to make a lattice. Brush strips with beaten egg yolk. Bake for 35-40 minutes until it turns a rich golden brown. Leave to cool in the tin for about 5 minutes before releasing the base.

DATE TRIANGLES
Makes 30

Pastry: 6 oz (175 g) butter or hard margarine
    4 oz (110 g) plain flour, sifted
    4 oz (110 g) self raising flour, sifted

3 oz (75 g) caster sugar
1 egg, beaten

Filling: 8 oz (225 g) stoned dates, chopped
    2 tbsp lemon juice

4 oz (110 g) dark brown sugar
4 tbsp water

Rub the butter or margarine into the flours until the mixture resembles fine breadcrumbs Stir in the sugar and beaten egg and bind into a firm dough. Wrap in clingfilm and chill for 20 minutes. Preheat the oven to 350°F/180°C/Gas Mk 4. Meanwhile put all the filling ingredients in a saucepan and simmer gently for 10 minutes, until the mixture is fairly thick and sticky. Remove pastry from fridge and use two-thirds of it to line a large, lightly greased Swiss roll tin. Spread over the filling and make a lattice topping with the remaining pastry. Bake in the centre of the oven for 35-40 minutes and leave in the tin to cool. Cut into triangles or squares.

TOFFEE SHORTCAKE
Makes 30

8 oz (225 g) butter, softened
6 oz (175 g) caster sugar
6 oz (175 g) flour, sifted

2 tbsp golden syrup
4 tbsp condensed milk
6 oz (175 g) chocolate

Preheat the oven to 350°F/180°C/Gas Mk 4. Cream together 4 oz (110 g) of the butter and 4 oz (110 g) of the caster sugar. Work in the flour to a stiff pastry. Press into a Swiss roll tin, prick well all over and bake for about 20 minutes. Gently dissolve the remaining 4 oz (110 g) butter and 2 oz (50 g) caster sugar with the golden syrup and condensed milk in a saucepan. Bring to the boil and boil without stirring for 5-10 minutes. Quickly spread over the cooked shortbread base and leave to cool. Melt the chocolate in a pan over hot water and then spread over the set caramel topping. Mark into 30 pieces before cooling completely.

ORANGE TART
Makes an 8 inch (20 cm) tart

Pastry:
6 oz (175 g) plain flour, sifted
pinch of salt
2 oz (50 g) butter or soft margarine

1 oz (25 g) lard
water to mix

Filling:
5 level tbsp orange marmalade
2 oz (50 g) soft margarine
2 oz (50 g) caster sugar
3 oz (75 g) self-raising flour

½ level tsp baking powder
1 large egg, beaten
thin strips of orange rind
to decorate

Sift the flour and salt into a bowl. Rub in the butter or margarine and the lard until the consistency resembles fine breadcrumbs. Stir in enough cold water to mix to a soft dough. Wrap in clingfilm and chill for 20 minutes. Preheat the oven to 350°F/180°C/Gas Mk 4. Roll dough out on a lightly floured surface and use it to line an 8 inch (20 cm) flan tin. Spread half the marmalade over the base of the flan. Beat together the soft margarine and caster sugar then sift in the flour and baking powder and bind with egg. Add grated orange rind and beat all the ingredients for about 2 minutes. Spread over the marmalade. Cook for 30-35 minutes until the sponge is firm to the touch. Cool. Melt the rest of the marmalade, brush it over the top and decorate with the thin strips of orange rind.

VIENNESE TARTS
Makes 9

6 oz (175 g) unsalted margarine or butter
6 oz (175 g) plain flour
2 oz (50 g) caster sugar
¼ tsp vanilla essence
2 level tbsp icing sugar, sifted
1-2 level tbsp redcurrant jelly

Prepare a large piping bag with a star nozzle and nine paper cases in a nine-hole bun tin. Preheat the oven to 350°F/180°C/Gas Mk 4. Beat the margarine or butter until soft and fluffy, then sift in the flour gradually, beating well after each addition. Beat in the sugar and vanilla essence. Spoon the mixture into the piping bag fitted with the star nozzle. Pipe the mixture in the shape of rosettes into the paper cases standing in a bun tray. Bake in centre of oven for 20-35 minutes or until light golden in colour. Cool on a wire tray. When cold dust with the icing sugar. Place a blob of jelly in the centre of each tart.

LEMON FINGERS
Makes 16

Pastry: 6 oz (175 g) plain flour, sifted
pinch of salt
2 oz (50 g) butter or soft margarine
1 oz (25 g) lard
water to mix

Filling: 4 oz (110 g) butter, melted
1 level tbsp cornflour
2 eggs, separated
4 oz (110 g) caster sugar
grated rind and juice of 2 large lemons

Sift the flour with the salt and rub in the butter or margarine until the mixture resembles fine breadcrumbs. Stir in enough cold water to mix to a soft dough, wrap in foil and chill for 20 minutes. Preheat the oven to 375° F/190°C/Gas Mk 5. Roll out the pastry and use to line a Swiss roll tin. Put the lemon rind and juice into a bowl, add the eggs, sugar, cornflour and melted butter and beat all together well with a rotary whisk for about half a minute then pour into the pastry lined tin. Bake just above the centre of the oven for 30 minutes, until the filling is set and the pastry cooked. Leave to cool in the tin before cutting into fingers.

CINNAMON TWISTS
Makes 6

2 oz (50 g) caster sugar
1 tsp ground cinnamon

7½ oz (215 g) packet frozen puff
pastry, thawed

Preheat the oven to 425°F/220°C/Gas Mk 7. Dampen a baking sheet. In a bowl, mix together the sugar and cinnamon and sprinkle half the amount on a flat surface. Roll out the thawed pastry on top of the sugar and cinnamon mixture. Sprinkle the remaining mixture on top of the pastry and roll it in. Roll to a 10 inch (25 cm) square. Divide and cut into twelve equal strips, moisten one end of each and twist to form a spiral. Press ends firmly together to seal. Place six twists on the baking sheet and bake for 10 minutes. Turn over and cook for 5 minutes until they are crisp and the sugar has caramelised. Remove and cool on a wire rack. Clean the baking sheet and cook the remaining twists in the same way. When cool, place in an airtight container.

SULTANA SQUARES
Makes 16

Pastry:
8 oz (225 g) plain flour, sifted
pinch of salt
2 oz (50 g) lard

2 oz (50 g) butter or soft margarine
water to mix

Filling:
4 oz (110 g) butter or margarine
4 oz (110 g) sultanas
4 oz (110 g) demerara sugar

1 egg
½ tsp vanilla essence
1 tbsp granulated sugar

Sift the flour together with a little pinch of salt and rub in the margarine and lard until the mixture resembles fine breadcrumbs. Stir in enough cold water to mix to a soft dough. Wrap in foil and chill for 20 minutes. Roll out half the dough on a lightly floured surface and use to line a Swiss roll tin. Prick the pastry base with a fork. Roll out the remaining pastry to a rectangle ½ inch (1 cm) wider than the tin. To make the filling, melt the butter or margarine and stir in the sugar, sultanas, egg and vanilla essence. Beat well and leave to cool, and then spread the filling over the pastry in the tin. Preheat the oven to 400°F/200°C/Gas Mk 6. Using a rolling pin, lift the pastry for the lid over the filling and cut away the excess pastry round the edges. Score the top with a sharp knife, then brush with a little milk and sprinkle with 1 tablespoon of granulated sugar. Bake for 30 minutes. Cool completely before cutting into squares.

STRAWBERRY PUFFS
Makes 18

2½ oz (75 g) plain flour, sifted
pinch of salt
2 oz (50 g) butter
5 fl oz (150 ml) water
2 eggs

8 oz (225 g) strawberries,
washed and hulled
5 fl oz (150 ml) clotted cream
1 tbsp caster sugar
1 tbsp icing sugar

Preheat the oven to 400°F/200°C/Gas Mk 6. Lightly grease two baking sheets. Put the fat and water in a saucepan and heat gently until the fat melts, then bring to the boil. Remove from heat and beat in the flour and salt until smooth. Leave to cool for 5 minutes. Whisk the eggs and gradually add into the flour mixture, beating well until it is shiny and smooth. Using large teaspoonfuls make eighteen separate mounds on the baking sheets and gently shape into rounds. Bake in the oven for 20-25 minutes, then remove from oven. Make a slit in the side of each puff to allow steam to escape. Return to oven and bake for 5 minutes to dry out. Remove from oven and transfer to a wire rack to cool. Place half the amount of strawberries in a bowl and add the cream and sugar. Mash well and beat until thick. Chop the remaining fruit into small pieces and fold into the mixture. Spoon into the puffs, sprinkle with icing sugar and eat soon after filling.

DATE AND ORANGE TART
Makes an 8 inch (20 cm) tart

Pastry:
8 oz (225 g) plain wholemeal flour
4 oz (110 g) butter or soft margarine
water to mix

Filling:
4 oz (110 g) stoned dates, soaked overnight in a little water
1 medium orange, cut into segments, pith removed

Rub the margarine or butter into the flour until the mixture resembles fine breadcrumbs. Stir in enough cold water to mix to a soft dough. Wrap in clingfilm and chill for 20 minutes. Preheat the oven to 400°F/200°C/Gas Mk 6. Roll out half of the dough on a lightly floured surface and use it to line an 8 inch (20 cm) flan tin. Prick the pastry base with a fork. Liquidise the dates and orange. Spread the mixture over the pastry then cover with the other half of the pastry rolled out. Press edge to seal. Bake for 35-45 minutes.

ALMOND SQUARES
Makes 12

3 oz (75 g) plain flour, sifted
pinch of salt
1 oz (25 g) caster sugar
2 oz (50 g) butter

Topping:
2 oz (50 g) butter
2 oz (50 g) caster sugar
1 large egg, beaten

3 oz (75 g) glacé cherries,
  washed and halved
icing sugar for dredging

2 oz (50 g) ground almonds
few drops almond essence

Preheat the oven to 375°F/190°C/Gas Mk 5. Sift the flour and salt
into a bowl and then mix in the sugar. Rub in the butter until the
mixture binds together. Place the dough in a lightly greased shallow
8 inch (20 cm) square cake tin and press it down flat to cover the base
of the tin. Arrange halved cherries all over the dough. To make the
topping, cream the butter and sugar together in a bowl until light and
fluffy. Beat in the egg. Add the almonds and a few drops of almond
essence. Mix well and spread evenly over the cherries. Bake in the
oven for 40 minutes until just set and golden. Remove from oven,
cool for a few minutes, then turn out onto a wire rack. Leave until
cold, sprinkle over icing sugar and cut into squares.

ALMOND AND CHERRY SLICES
Makes 14 slices

3 oz (75 g) plain flour
4 oz (110 g) butter or soft margarine
7 oz (200 g) caster sugar
6 oz (175 g) ground almonds
3 oz (75 g) self-raising flour

4 oz (110 g) glacé cherries,
  washed, dried and halved
2 eggs, beaten
almond essence
icing sugar

Preheat the oven to 350°F/180°C/Gas Mk 4. Sift the plain flour into a
basin and add half the butter cut into small pieces. Rub the butter into
the flour until it reaches fine breadcrumb stage, stir in 1 oz (25 g) caster sugar. Press this crumb mixture into a 7 inch (18 cm) tin. Mix the
remaining caster sugar, the ground almonds and sifted self-raising
flour in a bowl. Add half the cherries, the beaten egg and a few drops
of almond essence. Melt the remaining 2 oz (50 g) butter gently in a
pan and stir into the mixture. Spread this mixture over the crumb base
and top with the remaining glacé cherries. Bake in the centre of the
oven for about 1 hour or until set and golden brown on top. Cool on
a wire tray and dredge with icing sugar when cold and cut into slices.

JEANNIE'S BAKEWELL TART
Makes an 8 inch (20 cm) tart

Pastry:
3 oz (75 g) plain flour
3 oz (75 g) self raising flour

3 oz (75 g) hard margarine

Filling:
2 oz (50 g) butter or soft margarine
2 oz (50 g) caster sugar
1 large or 2 small eggs
3 oz (75 g) ground almonds

2 drops almond essence
apricot jam
a little milk

Preheat the oven to 350°F/180°C/Gas Mk 4. Sift the flours together and rub the margarine into the flour until the mixture resembles fine breadcrumbs. Stir in enough cold water to mix to a soft dough. Roll out on a lightly floured surface and use it to line an 8 inch (20 cm) flan tin. Prick the pastry base with a fork and spread with warmed sieved apricot jam. To make the filling, cream the butter or soft margarine with the caster sugar until light and fluffy. Beat in the egg or eggs and then gently fold in the ground almonds and the almond essence. Add 1 tablespoon milk if necessary. Pour into the pastry case and bake for 25-35 minutes until golden brown. Serve dusted with sifted icing sugar.

CINNAMON PLUM TART

12 oz (350 g) shortcrust pastry
1½ lb (675 g) plums
7 oz (200 g) caster sugar
1 tsp ground cinnamon
squeeze of lemon juice
1 oz (25 g) butter

Preheat the oven to 400°F/200°C/Gas Mk 4. Line a 9 inch (23 cm) sandwich tin, fluting the pastry at the edges. Halve and stone the plums and arrange cut side upwards over the pastry. Mix together the sugar and cinnamon and sprinkle half over the plums. Squeeze over the lemon juice and dot with butter. Bake in the oven for 40 minutes, then sprinkle with the remaining cinnamon sugar.

MINCEMEAT SLICES
Makes 12-14

8 oz (225 g) self-raising flour, sifted
4 oz (110 g) butter
4 oz (110 g) caster sugar
1 egg, beaten
2-3 tbsp milk
5-6 tbsp mincemeat
2 tbsp demerara sugar

Preheat the oven to 375°F/190°C/Gas Mk 5. Sift the flour into a bowl and rub in the butter until the mixture resembles fine breadcrumbs. Mix in the sugar and add the beaten egg and sufficient milk to mix to a soft dough. Divide the dough in half and press one half into a lightly greased 8 inch (20 cm) shallow square cake tin. Spread the mincemeat evenly over the dough leaving a narrow border around the edges. Roll out the other half of the dough and place over the mincemeat. Press down firmly, especially around the edges. Brush a little milk over the top and sprinkle on the demerara sugar. Bake for 35-40 minutes until well risen and firm. Remove from oven and leave to cool slightly, then cut into squares. When completely cold, remove from tin and store in an airtight container.

SUMMER FRUIT TARTS
Serves 8

½ oz (10 g) butter
½ oz (10 g) plain flour
5 tbsp milk
1 tbsp caster sugar
5 tbsp single cream
1 egg yolk

few drops vanilla essence
1 packet of 8 ready-made
* shortcrust tartlets*
12 oz (350 g) hulled strawberries,
* raspberries and loganberries*
3 tbsp redcurrant jelly

Melt the butter in a small saucepan, stir in the flour and cook for 1 minute. Gradually add the milk and beat until smooth. Cook for another minute. Beat in the sugar, cream and egg yolk, and cook very gently for a further minute. Remove from the heat and stir in a few of drops of vanilla essence to taste. Cover the surface of the mixture with a round of damp greaseproof paper to prevent a skin forming while it cools. Place a tartlet on each of eight individual serving plates and fill the centre with the cold custard, smoothing the tops. Arrange the mixed summer fruits on top of each tartlet. Warm the redcurrant jelly with 1 tablespoon water until melted. Brush this over the fruits to glaze and leave to cool completely. Serve within 2 hours.

GOOSEBERRY ALMOND TART

Makes 16 squares

Pastry:
4 oz (110 g) plain flour
3 oz (75 g) self raising flour
5 oz (150 g) hard margarine
¼ tsp salt
3 tbsp caster sugar
1 egg, beaten
1-2 tbsp milk

Filling:
1 lb (450 g) gooseberries, topped and tailed
1 pt (600 ml) water
3 oz (75 g) caster sugar
1 tbsp cornflour
4 oz (110 g) butter or soft margarine
4 oz (110 g) caster sugar
3 eggs, beaten
2 oz (50 g) ground almonds
2 drops almond essence
4 oz (110 g) self-raising flour
grated rind and juice of 1 lemon
a little milk
2 oz (50 g) flaked almonds

Rub the margarine into the flour and salt until the mixture resembles fine breadcrumbs, then stir in the sugar. Add the egg and work the mixture together with the fingertips, gradually adding enough milk to make a soft dough. Chill for 30 minutes. Meanwhile, cook the gooseberries in the water until just tender, then remove half with a slotted spoon and reserve. Mix the sugar and cornflour together and then add to the mixture in the pan. Mash until well mixed, then bring back to the boil, stirring, and cook until it thickens slightly. Set aside and allow to cool. Preheat the oven to 400°F/200°C/Gas Mk 6. Roll out the pastry on a lightly floured surface and use it to line a greased Swiss roll tin. Chill for 10 minutes .Cream the butter or margarine with the caster sugar until l light and fluffy. Beat in the eggs and then fold in the ground almonds and the almond essence. Stir in the flour and the lemon rind and juice then milk if needed to make a dropping consistency. Spread the mashed gooseberry purée over the pastry base. Spoon the almond mixture over, then scatter with the whole gooseberries and flaked almonds. Bake for 20 minutes, then reduce the heat to 350°F/180°C/Gas Mk 4 for 40 minutes. If the edges start to brown, cover with foil. Cool in the tin before cutting into squares.

BANBURY CAKES 1
Makes 15

8 oz (225 g) plain flour, sifted
pinch of salt
3 oz (75 g) lard, cut into small pieces
3 oz (75 g) hard margarine, cut into small pieces

Filling:
1 oz (25 g) margarine
2 level tbsp plain flour
½ level tsp ground nutmeg
4 oz (110 g) cleaned currants
1 oz (25 g) chopped mixed peel
2 oz (50 g) dark soft brown sugar
1 tbsp lemon juice
a little water
caster sugar for glaze

Sift the flour and salt together into a mixing bowl and rub in the fats. Mix in enough water to make a fairly soft dough. Turn onto a floured board and roll into a rectangle about 14 x 6 inches (35 x 15 cm). Fold into three by bring the bottom third over the centre third, then top third down over the other two pieces. Seal the edges with a rolling pin and turn the dough a quarter turn anti-clockwise, roll and fold once more. Re-seal the edges, wrap in foil and leave to rest in the fridge for 15 minutes. Repeat this complete process twice more, by which time the fat should be evenly distributed throughout the pastry. Re-wrap in foil and leave in the fridge while making the filling. Melt the margarine gently in a pan and stir in the flour. Cook for 1 minute. Remove from the heat and stir in the nutmeg, currants, peel, sugar and lemon juice and leave to cool. Preheat the oven to 425°F/220°C/Gas Mk 7. On a lightly floured surface roll out the pastry to ¼ inch (5 mm) thick and cut out fifteen rounds of pastry. Put the scraps one on top of another and re-roll, cutting out another three rounds. Place a teaspoon of filling in the centre of each round, dampen the edges with cold water and gather the edges together towards the centre. Turn the cakes over, so that all the joins are underneath, and roll each one gently into an oval about 4 inches (10 cm) long. Transfer to a baking tray and make two slits across the top. Brush with water and sprinkle with caster sugar. Bake for 20 minutes or until they are golden brown. Cool on a wire tray.

BANBURY CAKES 2
Makes about 12

1 large packet puff pastry
1 tbsp rum (optional)
1 egg white
caster sugar for dusting

Filling: 2½ oz (65 g) butter
½ tsp each allspice and nutmeg
4½ oz (125 g) currants or raisins

¼ tsp cinnamon
2 oz (50 g) chopped candied peel
2½ oz (75 g) caster sugar

Preheat the oven to 425°F/220°C/Gas Mk 7. Roll out the pastry on a floured board, cut out as many 7 inch (18 cm) circles as possible and chill on a tray. Make the filling by melting the butter over a low heat, remove from the heat and stir in the rest of the ingredients, mixing well and cool. Divide this mixture between the pastry circles, spreading it down the centre. Bring the sides of the pastry over, then the top and bottom to enclose the filling in an oval shape. Seal the edges with a little beaten egg white. Turn the cakes over, flattening them slightly with the palm of the hand. Put on baking tray and cut three slashes in the top of each cake with a sharp knife. Brush with the egg white and sprinkle with sugar. Bake in between the centre and top of the oven for about 15 minutes until the pastry is cooked and the glaze is a deep golden brown.

SLY CAKES
Makes 12-14

8 oz (225 g) packet of frozen puff
pastry, thawed
2 oz (50 g) chopped mixed peel

¼ tsp mixed spice
4 oz (110 g) currants
1 tbsp sugar for sprinkling

Preheat the oven to 425°F/220°C/Gas Mk 7. Lightly grease a baking sheet. Roll out the thawed pastry on a flat lightly floured surface to a 12 inches (30 cm) square. Brush with a little water. Mix the currants, peel, spice and sugar in a bowl. Arrange evenly over half the pastry, then fold over the other half of the pastry. Roll gently until the fruit mixture can just be seen through the pastry. Cut into triangle shapes and sprinkle with sugar. Carefully transfer to the baking sheet and bake for 10-15 minutes until risen and golden. Transfer to a wire rack to cool.

ALMOND APRICOT TART
Makes a 9 inch (23 cm) flan

Pastry:
3 oz (75 g) plain flour, sifted
3 oz (75 g) self raising flour, sifted

3 oz (75 g) hard margarine

Filling:
8 oz (225 g) no-soak dried apricots
8 fl oz (250 ml) boiling water
2 oz (50 g) soft margarine
2 eggs
1 oz (25 g) wholemeal self-raising flour

2 tbsp orange juice
2 tbsp clear honey
1 oz (25 g) flaked almonds
1 tsp icing sugar
4 oz (110 g) ground almonds

Preheat the oven to 400°F/200°C/Gas Mk 6. Sift the flours together with a pinch of salt and rub in the margarine until the mixture resembles fine breadcrumbs. Stir in enough cold water to mix to a soft dough. Wrap in clingfilm and chill for 20 minutes. Roll out on a floured surface and line a 9 inch (23 cm) flan tin. Prick the pastry base with a fork, line with foil and baking beans and bake for 10 minutes. Remove foil and beans and bake for 5 minutes more. To make the filling, soak the apricots in the boiling water for 5 minutes, then simmer for 5 minutes. Blend to a purée and cool. Cream the margarine until light and fluffy. Beat in the eggs and then fold in the flour, ground almonds, orange juice and honey. Spread the apricot purée over the pastry base and spoon the almond mixture on top. Scatter over flaked almonds and bake for 25 minutes. Dust with sifted icing sugar.

LEMON PUFFS
Makes 9

8 oz (225 g) pkt puff pastry

Filling:
grated rind of 1 lemon
2 oz (50 g) caster sugar
2 tbsp double cream

1 egg
1 oz (25 g) ground almonds
2 oz (50 g) margarine, melted

Preheat the oven to 400°F/200°C/Gas Mk 6. Roll out the pastry to a 10 inch (25 cm) square. Using a cutter, cut out nine rounds and use these to line a nine-hole patty tin. Knead the trimmings together and roll out again. Cut into ⅛ inch (3 mm) wide strips. Beat together all the filling ingredients and divide between the patty tins, filling each pastry case about two-thirds full. Lay the pastry strips over the filling in a lattice pattern, trimming the edges with a sharp knife. Bake towards the top of a preheated oven for 15 minutes.

APPLE SLICE
Serves 4

1 lb (450 g) cooking apples
squeeze of lemon juice
7½ oz (210 g) pkt frozen puff pastry
2 oz (50 g) caster sugar

Preheat the oven to 400°F/200°C/Gas Mk 6. Peel, core and thinly slice the apples and place in a bowl of cold water to which a squeeze of lemon juice has been added. Roll out the pastry on a lightly floured board to 8½ inches (21 cm) square. Lift onto a damp baking sheet and prick all over with a fork. Drain the apples and arrange attractively over the pastry to within 1 inch (2.5 cm) of the edge. Sprinkle with caster sugar and bake in a preheated oven for about 25 minutes or until the apples are soft and the pastry is golden brown. Melt the apricot jam with 1 tablespoon of water in a small saucepan and use to brush over the apples. Serve warm or cold with whipped cream.

WALNUT SQUARES
Makes 24

9 oz (250 g) plain flour
6 oz (175 g) margarine
1½ oz (40 g) caster sugar

Topping:
3 eggs
9 oz (250 g) soft brown sugar
3 level tbsp plain flour
½ level tsp baking powder

4 oz (110 g) chopped walnuts
1 oz (25 g) desiccated coconut
½ tsp vanilla essence

Preheat the oven to 375°F/190°C/Gas Mk 5. Sift the plain flour into a bowl and add the margarine cut into small pieces. Rub until the mixture resembles fine breadcrumbs. Stir in 1½ oz (40 g) sugar. Press into base of a large Swiss roll tin. Cook in the centre of the oven for 5 minutes. For the topping whisk the eggs and sugar together until light and fluffy. Sift the flour with the baking powder and fold into the egg mixture with the walnuts, coconut and vanilla essence. Spread over the crumb mixture in the tin and cook for a further 25-30 minutes until golden brown on top. Leave to cool on a wire tray and then cut into squares.

COFFEE FUDGE SQUARES
Makes 24 squares

Base:
4 oz (110 g) soft margarine
4 oz (110 g) caster sugar
2 eggs, beaten
1 oz (25 g) hazelnuts, chopped, or mixed nuts, chopped
1 tbsp coffee essence
4 oz (110 g) self-raising flour
½ level tsp baking powder

Fudge icing:
2 oz (50 g) margarine
6 oz (175 g) icing sugar
1 tbsp milk
1 tbsp coffee essence
4 oz (110 g) toasted hazelnuts, chopped, or mixed nuts, chopped
24 whole hazelnuts

Grease and line a Swiss roll tin. Preheat the oven to 325°F/170°C/ Gas Mk 3. Place the margarine, sugar, eggs, chopped nuts and coffee essence in a bowl. Sift in the flour and baking powder and beat together until the mixture is soft and drops from a spoon, then turn into the tin and smooth the top level. Bake in centre of the oven for 40-45 minutes until the centre is firm. Leave in the tin to cool, then turn out and remove the greaseproof paper. Trim away the edges with a sharp knife and cut into 24 squares. To make the fudge icing, place the margarine in a bowl and gradually beat in the icing sugar, milk and coffee essence. Spread the icing thinly over the top and sides of the squares. Put the chopped nuts on a plate and press the covered cakes into the nuts until they are evenly coated. Top each cake with a whole hazelnut.

APPLE STRUDEL

Strudel:
8 oz (225 g) plain flour
pinch of salt
1 egg

1 tbsp oil
lukewarm water
icing sugar for dusting

Filling:
1 lb (450 g) apples, peeled,
cored and thinly sliced
2 oz (50 g) walnuts, chopped
2 oz (50 g) sultanas

2 tsp mixed spice
2 oz (50 g) soft brown sugar
2 tbsp breadcrumbs
2½ oz (65 g) butter

Preheat the oven to 425°F/220°C/Gas Mark 7. Sieve the flour and salt into a bowl and drop the egg into the centre. Mix the oil with 6 tbsp lukewarm water and use the liquid to mix the flour and egg to a smooth dough. Work the dough on a board until it is smooth and elastic. Cover with a cloth and rest the dough while preparing the filling. Mix the sliced apple with the nuts, sultanas, spice and sugar. Fry the breadcrumbs in 1 oz (25 g) butter until golden brown. Melt the remaining butter and keep warm. Put a clean teatowel on a flat work surface and dust with flour. Roll out the dough on the cloth, then stretch it as thin as possible, until it is almost transparent. Trim away any thicker edges. Brush the melted butter over the dough, then sprinkle over the breadcrumbs. Spread the apple mixture evenly over the dough. Using the cloth to lift the dough, roll it into a long sausage shape, then bend it into a horseshoe shape and place it on a baking sheet. Brush over the top of the strudel with any remaining melted butter and bake in the oven for 30 minutes until crisp and golden. Dust with icing sugar and serve cut into slices.

RHUBARB BAKE
Makes 12 squares

For the pastry:
10 oz (300 g) plain
  flour, sifted
½ level tsp cinnamon
¼ level tsp salt

6 oz (175 g) soft margarine
4 oz (110 g) caster sugar
1 egg, beaten

Filling:
1 level tbsp cornflour
2 tbsp lemon juice
6 oz (175 g) granulated sugar

1 lb (450 g) rhubarb, trimmed
  and cut into 1 in (2.5 cm) lengths

Rub the margarine into the flour, cinnamon and salt until the mixture resembles fine breadcrumbs. Stir in the sugar and beaten egg and bind into a firm dough. Wrap in clingfilm and chill for 20 minutes. Preheat the oven to 400°F/200°C/Gas Mk 6. Meanwhile mix the cornflour to a paste with the lemon juice in a saucepan. Stir in the rhubarb and sugar and bring to the boil, stirring continuously. Reduce the heat, cover and simmer for 15 minutes, then allow to cool. Remove pastry from fridge and cut in half. Grate half over the tin and spread evenly over the base. Spread over the rhubarb filling and grate the remaining pastry over the top. Make sure the topping goes right to the corners of the tin to prevent filling seeping, but do not flatten it. Bake in the centre of the oven for 30-35 minutes and leave in the tin to cool before cutting into squares.

ALMOND TART
Makes a 9 inch (23 cm) flan

Pastry:
6 oz (175 g) butter
6 oz (175 g) plain flour, sifted

3 tbsp cold water
4 tbsp apricot jam

Filling:
4 oz (110 g) butter
4 oz (110 g) caster sugar
2 eggs
4 oz (110 g) cake crumbs
   (crumbled trifle sponge
   or Madeira cake)

4 oz (110 g) ground almonds
few drops almond essence

Preheat the oven to 400°F/200°C/Gas Mk 6. Rub the softened butter into the flour until it resembles fine breadcrumbs. Add the cold water and mix to a soft dough. Knead the dough lightly on a floured board and roll out to fit a 9 inch (23 cm) flan tin. Reserve the trimmings and spread the base with apricot jam. To make the filling, cream the butter and sugar together until soft and fluffy, then beat in the eggs, cake crumbs, ground almonds and almond essence. Spread over the pastry and decorate with shapes cut from the trimmings. Bake just below the centre of the oven for 30 minutes, then reduce the heat to 325°F/ 170°C/Gas Mk 3 and cook for a further 30 minutes. Cool in the tin.

CURD TART
Makes an 8 inch (20 cm) flan

Pastry:
6 oz (175 g) plain flour
pinch of salt
2 oz (50 g) butter or hard margarine
1 oz (25 g) lard
water to mix

Filling:
8 oz (225 g) cream cheese
2 eggs, separated
2 oz (50 g) caster sugar
grated rind of 1 lemon
2 oz (50 g) currants
pinch nutmeg
thin strips of lemon rind to decorate

Sift the flour together with the salt and rub in the margarine until the mixture resembles fine breadcrumbs. Stir in enough cold water to mix to a soft dough. Wrap in clingfilm and chill for 20 minutes. Preheat the oven to 400°F/200°C/Gas Mk 6, roll out the dough on a lightly floured surface and use it to line an 8 inch (20 cm) flan tin. Prick the pastry base with a fork. To make the filling, beat together the cream cheese, egg yolks, sugar and grated lemon rind. Whisk the egg whites until stiff and then fold into the egg mixture with a metal spoon, together with the currants. Spoon into the pastry case and sprinkle with grated nutmeg. Bake for 15 minutes, then reduce the oven temperature to 350°F/180°C /Gas Mk 4 and cook for a further 15 minutes or until golden and firm to the touch. Serve cold decorated with fine strips of lemon rind.

BISCUITS

FIG COOKIES
Makes 36

4 oz (110 g) butter
4 oz (110 g) soft light brown sugar
1 egg, beaten
1 tbsp clear honey
8 oz (225 g) self-raising flour
4 oz (110 g) dried figs, chopped

Preheat the oven to 350°F/180°C/Gas Mk 4. Grease and flour three baking sheets. Cream the butter and sugar in a bowl until light and fluffy. Beat in the egg and honey gradually. Sift in the flour and gently fold into the mixture. Mix in the figs and then arrange spoonfuls of the mixture on the sheets, leaving room for each cookie to spread. Gently flatten each one. Bake in the oven for 10-12 minutes until the edges are light brown. Leave to cool before transferring to wire racks.

SESAME COOKIES
Makes 36

1½ oz (40 g) sesame seeds
3½ oz (90 g) muesli (untoasted type)
8 oz (225 g) sugar
4 oz (110 g) plain flour
pinch of salt
4 oz (110 g) butter
1 tbsp golden syrup
1½ tsp bicarbonate of soda
2 tbsp boiling water

Preheat the oven to 300°F/150°C/Gas Mk 2. Place the sesame seeds in a frying pan and toast over a low heat until golden. In a large bowl, mix together the muesli, sugar, flour, salt and sesame seeds. Melt the butter in a small saucepan, and mix in the syrup. Remove from heat, stir in the soda and boiling water. Pour into the flour mixture and mix until well blended. Place spoonfuls of mixture on greased baking sheets, leaving room for the cookies to spread. Cook in the oven for 20 minutes until golden. Leave on the baking sheets for a few minutes to cool, then transfer to wire racks using a spatula.

SPICE BISCUITS
Makes 36

4 oz (110 g) butter
7 oz (200 g) caster sugar
1 egg, beaten
2 tsp milk
8 oz (225 g) plain flour
1 tsp bicarbonate of soda
1 tsp ground cinnamon
¼ tsp ground nutmeg
pinch of ground cloves
3 oz (75 g) currants

Cream the butter in a bowl with 6 oz (175 g) of the sugar and beat well together until light and fluffy. Beat in the egg and milk. Add the remaining ingredients except the 1 oz (25 g) of sugar and mix well. Cover the bowl and chill for 30 minutes. Preheat the oven to 375°F/190°C/Gas Mk 5. Roll out the dough thinly on a floured surface. Sprinkle with the remaining sugar and cut into shapes about 2 inches (5 cm) in length. Place on greased baking sheets and bake in the oven for 8 minutes until lightly browned. Cool on a wire rack.

ALMOND CRISPS
Makes 24

4 oz (110 g) butter
3 oz (75 g) caster sugar
1 egg yolk
few drops of almond essence
5 oz (150 g) self-raising flour
3 oz (75 g) almonds, chopped

Preheat the oven to 375°F/190°C/Gas Mk 5. Cream the butter and sugar in a bowl until light and fluffy. Beat in the egg yolk and almond essence, then gradually beat in the flour. Form 24 small balls from the dough. Roll the balls in the chopped almonds until they are completely coated. Arrange well apart on greased baking sheets and bake in the oven for 15-20 minutes until golden. Place on wire rack to cool.

SUGARY RINGS
Makes 20

6 oz (175 g) plain wholemeal flour
¼ tsp bicarbonate of soda
¼ tsp salt
2 oz (50 g) light soft brown sugar
3 oz (75 g) butter, cut into pieces
4 oz (110 g) currants
2 oz (50 g) oat flakes
1 egg, beaten

Sift the flour and soda in a bowl with the salt and stir in the sugar.
Add the butter and rub in until mixture resembles fine breadcrumbs.
Mix in the currants and oat flakes, followed by the egg. Add about
1 tablespoon of water to bind to a dough and knead until smooth.
Cover the bowl and leave in a cool place for 30 minutes. Roll out the
dough thinly on a floured flat surface and cut into rounds using a
2 inch (5 cm) cutter. Use a 1 inch (2.5 cm) cutter to remove centres.
With a palette knife, transfer the rings to a greased baking sheet. (The
centres can be re-rolled and used to make more rings.) Chill for
20 minutes. Preheat the oven to 350°F/180°C/Gas Mk 4. Bake for
15 minutes until golden and firm. Cool on a wire rack.

APRICOT OAT CRUNCHIES
Makes 12

3 oz (75 g) self-raising flour
3 oz (75 g) rolled porridge oats
3 oz (75 g) demerara sugar
4 oz (110 g) butter
4 oz (110 g) no-soak dried apricots, chopped

Preheat the oven to 350°F/180°C/Gas Mk 4. Sift the flour into a
bowl, add the oats and sugar and mix well. Cut in the butter and rub
in until the mixture resembles fine breadcrumbs. Press half of the
mixture into a lightly greased shallow Swiss roll tin. Spread the
chopped apricots on top and sprinkle on the remaining oat mixture,
pressing down firmly. Bake for 25 minutes until golden brown. Leave
to cool in the tin for about 1 hour. Cut into bars.

SEMI-SWEET OATMEAL BISCUITS
Makes 14 squares

4 oz (110 g) margarine
2 oz (50 g) sugar
4 oz (110 g) flour
a good pinch of salt
4 oz (110 g) fine oatmeal
milk to mix
2 oz (50 g) almonds, finely chopped

Preheat the oven to 375°F/190°C/Gas Mk 5. Cream the margarine and sugar together in a bowl. Sift in the flour and salt, then add the oatmeal. Mix well and add enough milk to make a firm dough. Roll out on a floured surface and press into a greased 7 inch (17.5 cm) sandwich tin. Sprinkle the almonds on top and bake for 20-25 minutes. Leave to cool in the tin, then cut into squares.

CHOCOLATE PEPPERMINT CREAM COOKIES
Makes 10

5 oz (150 g) plain flour
2 tbsp cocoa powder
3 oz (75 g) butter
3 oz (75 g) caster sugar
vanilla essence
beaten egg

Peppermint butter cream:
1½ oz (40 g) butter
3 oz (75 g) icing sugar
peppermint essence

Preheat the oven to 375°F/190°C/Gas Mk 5. Sift the flour and cocoa powder into a bowl and rub in the butter until mixture resembles fine breadcrumbs. Add the sugar and a few drops of vanilla essence and mix to a stiff paste with the beaten egg. Roll out thinly on a floured surface. Cut into rounds with a 2 inch (5 cm) plain cutter. Remove the centres from half the biscuits, using a 1 inch (2.5 cm) plain cutter. Place all the biscuits on greased baking sheets and bake for 10-15 minutes. Leave to cool and make the icing. Cream the butter and icing sugar together in a bowl until light and fluffy. Add a few drops of peppermint essence. Spread the mixture onto the cooled whole biscuits and place the open rounds on top.

MAPLE WALNUT BISCUITS
Makes 14

4 oz (110 g) margarine
3 oz (75 g) sugar
2 tsp maple syrup
7 oz (200 g) plain flour, sifted
1 tsp strong coffee
2 oz (50 g) walnuts, chopped

Preheat the oven to 375°F/190°C/Gas Mk 5. In a bowl, cream the margarine, sugar and syrup. Sift in the flour, add the coffee and walnuts to the mixture and knead together. Add a few drops of milk if the mixture is too dry. On a floured surface, carefully roll out the mixture thinly. Cut into round shapes with a fluted cutter. Arrange on a lightly greased and floured baking tray and bake for 10 minutes. Leave to cool on a wire tray, then store in an airtight tin. Serve dusted with icing sugar.

DANISH BROWN BISCUITS
Makes 24

4 oz (110 g) golden syrup
2 oz (50 g) brown sugar
1 oz (25 g) white cooking fat
1 tsp ground cloves
1 tsp cinnamon
½ tsp ground ginger
grated rind of ½ orange
¼ tsp bicarbonate of soda
6 oz (175 g) plain flour, sifted
chopped almonds

Preheat the oven to 375°F/190°C/Gas Mk 5. Place the syrup, sugar, cooking fat, cloves, cinnamon, ginger and orange rind in a saucepan, and heat gently until the ingredients have dissolved. Leave to cool slightly and then mix in the bicarbonate of soda. Sift the flour into a bowl, then pour on the mixture from the saucepan. Stir well and form into a dough. Roll out thinly on a floured surface and cut into finger shapes. Arrange on a greased baking sheet. Brush the tops with milk and sprinkle over the chopped almonds. Bake in the oven for 8-10 minutes. Transfer to a wire rack to cool.

COFFEE WALNUT BISCUITS
Makes 12

4 oz (110 g) margarine
3 oz (75 g) sugar
2 oz (50 g) walnuts, finely chopped
6 oz (175 g) plain flour, sifted
1 tbsp strong coffee liquid
extra chopped walnuts for decoration
some milk

Preheat the oven to 375°F/190°C/Gas Mk 5. Cream together the margarine and sugar in a bowl. Mix in the flour and coffee. Add the walnuts to the mixture. Knead well together, adding a few drops of milk if the mixture is too dry. Roll out thinly on a floured surface. Cut into round shapes with a fluted cutter. Arrange on a lightly greased and floured baking tray. Brush with a little milk and sprinkle over some chopped walnuts. Bake in the oven for 10 minutes. Leave to cool on wire tray, then store in an airtight tin.

ANZACS
Makes 20

5 oz (150 g) butter
1 tbsp golden syrup
1 tsp bicarbonate of soda
2 tbsp boiling water
4 oz (110 g) plain flour
4 oz (110 g) rolled oats
4 oz (110 g) sugar
4 oz (110 g) raisins

Preheat the oven to 300°F/150°C/Gas Mk 2. Melt the butter and syrup together. Dissolve the bicarbonate of soda in the boiling water and add to the mixture. Mix together the flour, oats, sugar and raisins and pour the butter and syrup mixture over the dry ingredients. Mix well. Place teaspoonfuls of the mixture on a greased baking tray, leaving room for the biscuits to spread. Bake in the oven for about 15 minutes. Leave on the tray for 5 minutes before transferring to wire racks to cool.

CHOC AND CHERRY BISCUITS
Makes 12

4 oz (110 g) margarine
2 oz (50 g) soft brown sugar
1 tbsp clear honey
1 oz (25 g) glacé cherries, chopped
1 oz (25 g) chocolate chips
4 oz (110 g) plain flour, sifted

Beat the margarine with the sugar and honey until light and fluffy. Fold in the cherries, chocolate chips and flour with a metal spoon. Place teaspoons of the mixture on a greased baking tray, spacing them well apart to allow for spreading. Bake in the middle of the oven for 15-18 minutes until golden. Remove from the oven, leave for a few moments on the baking tray then lift onto a wire cooling rack.

COCONUT COOKIES
Makes 16

8 oz (225 g) self-raising flour, sifted
4 oz (110 g) margarine
6 oz (175 g) caster sugar
2 oz (50 g) desiccated coconut
2 medium eggs, beaten

Preheat the oven to 375°F/190°C/Gas Mk 5. Rub the margarine into the flour until it resembles fine breadcrumbs. Stir in the caster sugar and desiccated coconut and mix to a firm dough with the beaten eggs. Roll the mixture into small balls and place on greased baking trays, leaving plenty of space in between each ball. Flatten each biscuit lightly with a fork. Bake near the top of the oven for 10-12 minutes or until golden brown.

WHOLEWHEAT SHORTIES
Makes 16

8 oz (225 g) wholewheat flour
pinch of salt
6 oz (175 g) butter
4 oz (110 g) soft brown sugar

Preheat the oven to 375°F/190°C/Gas Mk 5. Rub the butter into the flour and salt until the mixture resembles fine breadcrumbs. Stir in the sugar and knead with your hands until a soft dough is obtained. Roll out to ½ inch (10 mm) thick on a floured board. Press into a greased, shallow, oblong baking tin and prick all over with a fork. Bake on the middle shelf of the oven for 25 minutes until golden brown. Mark out fingers with a sharp knife and allow to cool in the tin. Remove and leave to cool completely on a wire rack before cutting.

AFGHANS
Makes 24

7 oz (200 g) butter
3 oz (75 g) caster sugar
8 oz (225 g) self-raising flour ,sifted
1 tbsp cocoa powder, sifted
1 tbsp desiccated coconut
2 oz (50 g) cornflakes

Icing:
2 oz (50 g) plain chocolate
4 oz (110 g) icing sugar
2 tbsp milk
water
vanilla essence

Beat the butter and sugar together until thick and fluffy. Fold in the sifted flour and cocoa, add the coconut then the cornflakes and mix thoroughly. Put teaspoonfuls of the mixture, spaced well apart, on greased baking trays and bake for about 20 minutes When cold, top with chocolate icing. To make the icing, chop the chocolate and put into a bowl with the milk and water. Stand the bowl over a saucepan of hot water, and, when the chocolate has melted, stir in the sifted icing sugar and vanilla essence to taste. Beat thoroughly until smooth.

BOURBON BISCUITS
Makes 12

2 oz (50 g) margarine
2 oz (50 g) caster sugar
1 egg, beaten
2 oz (50 g) plain flour
1 oz (25 g) cocoa powder
few drops vanilla essence
2 oz (50 g) semolina

Filling:
½ oz (15 g) margarine
1 tsp cocoa powder
1 heaped tbsp icing sugar

Preheat the oven to 375°F/190°C/Gas Mk 5. Cream the margarine and sugar together until light and fluffy, then beat in the egg a little at a time. Sift the flour and cocoa powder together and stir in the vanilla and semolina. Lightly stir, then knead the dry ingredients into the creamed mixture, adding a little water, if necessary, to make a firm dough. Roll out on a board and cut into about 24 fingers with a sharp knife. Prick with a fork and sprinkle with granulated sugar before baking. Place on a greased baking tray and bake for about 20 minutes until crisp. Lift onto a wire tray to cool. To make the filling, melt the margarine and sieve in the cocoa and sugar a little at a time. Use to sandwich the biscuits together.

CHOCOLATE MACAROONS
Makes 10

2 egg whites
4 oz (110 g) caster sugar
2½ oz (60 g) drinking chocolate
4 oz (110 g) ground almonds
1 oz (25 g) margarine, melted
10 blanched almonds

Line a baking tray with greaseproof paper, or grease lightly. Whisk the egg whites until stiff, then fold in the dry ingredients (except the blanched almonds) and melted margarine. Place in small heaps spaced well apart on the baking tray, and press a whole blanched almond on each. Bake for about 20 minutes or until firm to the touch. Cool for a few moments on the tray and then lift onto cooling racks.

CHOCOLATE CREAM FINGERS
Makes 12

3 oz (75 g) margarine
3 oz (75 g) caster sugar
1 egg, beaten
5 oz (150 g) self-raising flour, sifted
1 oz (25 g) cocoa powder
pinch of salt
milk to mix
few drops vanilla essence

Preheat the oven to 400°F/200°C/Gas Mk 6. Cream the margarine and sugar together until light and fluffy and beat in the egg a little at a time. Sift the dry ingredients into the cream mixture and mix to a very stiff dropping consistency with the milk and vanilla essence. Using a large star pipe in a forcing bag, pipe in lengths onto a greased baking tray. Bake for 10-15 minutes, then leave to cool. When cold, sandwich together with white or chocolate butter cream, and dip the ends in chocolate icing.

PEPPERNUT BISCUITS
Makes 14

4 oz (110 g) butter, softened
4 oz (110 g) caster sugar
2 eggs, beaten
4 oz (110 g) plain flour, sifted
¼ tsp salt
¼ tsp bicarbonate of soda
½ tsp each black pepper, grated nutmeg, ground cloves and allspice
1 tsp ground cinnamon
1 oz (25 g) ground almonds
9 oz (250 g) mixed candied peel, chopped

Preheat the oven to 350°F/180°C/Gas Mk 4. Cream the butter and sugar in a bowl until fluffy. Beat in the eggs and add the sifted flour, salt, bicarbonate of soda and all the spices. Mix well and beat in the almonds and peel. Drop spoonfuls of the mixture onto greased baking sheets leaving room for the biscuits to spread and cook in the oven for 10-12 minutes until the tops are brown and the edges are crisp. Leave to cool for a few minutes on the sheets, then transfer to wire racks.

MARMALADE CHEWS
Makes 16

3 oz (75 g) butter, softened
5 oz (150 g) caster sugar
1 beaten egg
5 oz (150 g) thick marmalade
6 oz (175 g) plain flour, sifted
1½ tsp baking powder

Preheat the oven to 375°F/190°C/Gas Mk 5. Cream together the butter and sugar in a bowl, then gradually beat in the egg and marmalade. Sift the flour and baking powder into the bowl and mix well. Extra flour or marmalade can be added if mixture is either too soft or too dry. Place spoonfuls of the mixture onto greased baking sheets, leaving room for the biscuits to spread. Cook in the oven for 8 minutes until the biscuits are firm underneath and golden brown on top. Leave to cool on sheets for a few minutes, before transferring to wire racks.

CHOCOLATE KISSES
Makes 12

1 oz (25 g) plain chocolate
7 oz (200 g) caster sugar
2 egg whites
½ tsp vanilla essence
¼ tsp cream of tartar
3 tbsp salted crisp savoury biscuits, crushed

Preheat the oven to 350°F/180°C/Gas Mk 4. Put the chocolate and 2 oz (50 g) of the sugar in a small bowl placed over a saucepan of hot water and stir until chocolate has melted. Remove the bowl from the saucepan and put aside to cool. In a separate bowl, beat the egg whites until stiff. Add the cream of tartar, vanilla essence and remaining sugar and beat well. Fold in the melted chocolate and the crushed biscuits. Place spoonfuls of the mixture on greased baking sheets, leaving room for the biscuits to spread. Cook for 10-12 minutes, until a glazed puff forms on top of the biscuits. Leave to cool for a few minutes on the trays, then transfer to wire racks using a spatula.

MELTING MOMENTS
Makes 24

4 oz (110 g) butter
3 oz (75 g) caster sugar
1 egg yolk
few drops vanilla essence
5 oz (150 g) self-raising flour
1 oz (25 g) crushed cornflakes

Preheat the oven to 375°F/190°C/Gas Mk 5. In a bowl, cream together the butter and sugar until fluffy. Beat in the egg yolk and add the vanilla essence. Gradually stir in the flour and beat well until a smooth dough forms. Make 24 small balls from the dough and then roll them in the cornflakes until well coated. Arrange on greased baking sheets and cook for 15-20 minutes. Cool on the baking sheets for a few minutes, then transfer to wire racks.

AMARETTI BISCUITS
Makes 24

4 oz (110 g) ground almonds
½ oz (15 g) ground rice
8 oz (225 g) caster sugar
2 egg whites
½ tsp almond essence
about 25 split almonds

Preheat the oven to 350°F/180°C/Gas Mk 4. In a bowl, mix together the ground almonds, ground rice and sugar. Beat in the egg whites and almond flavouring until smooth. Place the mixture into a piping bag fitted with a ½ inch (10 mm) plain nozzle and pipe small rounds onto baking sheets lined with rice paper. Leave room for the biscuits to spread. Place a split almond on top of each biscuit. Cook in the oven for 20 minutes until crisp and golden. Transfer to wire racks to cool. Cut off rice paper.

WINE BISCUITS
Makes 30

6 oz (175 g) plain flour
pinch of salt
4 oz (110 g) unsalted butter
3 oz (75 g) caster sugar
1 egg yolk
1 tbsp dry sherry

Topping:
1 egg white, lightly beaten
caster sugar
flaked almonds

Sift the flour and add the salt. Beat the butter and sugar in a bowl until soft. Beat the egg yolk and sherry together in a cup, then beat into the butter and sugar mixture. Add half the quantity of flour and salt to the mixture, mixing to a paste. Gradually beat in the remaining flour to mix to a soft dough. Place on a floured surface and form into a roll about 2 inches (5 cm) in diameter. Chill for a few hours wrapped in kitchen foil. Preheat the oven to 375°F/190°C/Gas Mk 5. Cut the roll into slices and arrange on greased baking sheets. Brush each one with the egg white and sprinkle with flaked almonds and caster sugar. Cook for 10-12 minutes until golden brown. Leave to cool on the baking sheets for 5 minutes, then transfer to wire racks.

ALMOND MACAROONS
Makes 20

4 oz (110 g) ground almonds
6 oz (175 g) caster sugar
2 egg whites, lightly beaten
¼ tsp almond essence
granulated sugar

Preheat the oven to 350°F/180°C/Gas Mk 4. Mix together the almonds and sugar, then beat in the egg whites, followed by the almond essence. Beat well until smooth. Place small mounds of the mixture onto baking sheets lined with baking parchment paper and sprinkle granulated sugar on top of each macaroon. Bake for 15 minutes until firm. Cool for a few minutes, then lift off from the paper and place on wire racks to cool completely.

GINGER MELTING MOMENTS
Makes 20

4 oz (110 g) butter
3 oz (75 g) caster sugar
1 egg yolk
1 tsp grated orange zest
5 oz (150 g) self-raising flour, sifted
1½ tsp ground ginger
3 tbsp bran breakfast cereal flakes, crushed

Mix together the sugar and butter in a bowl, then beat in the egg yolk and orange zest. Gradually mix in the flour and ginger and beat until smooth. Place the crushed cereal in a bowl. Shape the dough into small balls and roll in the cereal until well coated. Grease and flour two baking sheets. Arrange the balls on the baking sheets spaced well apart to allow for spreading. Bake for 15 minutes until golden brown. Leave to cool on the sheets before transferring to a wire rack.

TUILES
Makes 8

2 oz (50 g) almonds, flaked
2 oz (50 g) caster sugar
1 egg white
1 tbsp plain flour
rind of ½ lemon, finely grated

Preheat the oven to 425°F/220°C/Gas Mk 7. Put all the ingredients in a bowl and mix together thoroughly. Place teaspoonfuls on a greased and floured baking sheet, leaving room for the biscuits to spread. Cook for 6-8 minutes until golden brown. Using a palette knife, gently remove from the baking sheet and fold over a rolling pin to form them into curved shapes. Slide onto a wire tray and leave until crisp.

ROLLED OAT COOKIES
Makes 36

4 oz (110 g) butter
4 oz (110 g) demerara sugar
2 oz (50 g) golden syrup
4 oz (110 g) self-raising flour, sifted
½ tsp bicarbonate of soda
pinch of salt
4 oz (110 g) rolled oats
1 oz (25 g) walnuts, finely chopped

Put the butter, sugar and syrup in a saucepan and stir well over low heat until all the ingredients are blended. Remove from the heat and leave to cool slightly. Sift the flour, bicarbonate of soda and salt into a bowl and stir in the rolled oats and walnuts. Pour in the melted butter mixture and beat to a dough. Form about 36 small balls from the dough and arrange on greased baking sheets, leaving room for them to spread. Cook in the oven for 15 minutes until lightly browned. Leave to cool on the baking sheets for 5 minutes, then transfer to wire racks.

GIANT RUM AND RAISIN RANCH COOKIES
Makes 12

4 oz (110 g) California raisins
2 tbsp rum
4 oz (110 g) self-raising flour, sifted
4 oz (110 g) fine semolina
4 oz (110 g) butter
4 oz (110 g) demerara sugar
finely grated rind of ½ orange
1 egg, beaten
1 tbsp milk

Put the raisins in a bowl, pour over the rum and leave to soak overnight. Sift together the flour and semolina, then rub in the butter until the mixture resembles fine breadcrumbs. Stir in the sugar, orange rind, raisins and any remaining rum. Preheat the oven to 375°F/190°C/Gas Mk 5. Whisk the egg and milk together and mix into the dry mixture until a stiff dough forms. Divide the mixture into twelve portions and shape these into large rounds. Place on lightly greased baking trays and flatten slightly. Cook in the oven for 15 minutes or until just firm to the touch and golden. Cool slightly and transfer to wire racks to cool completely.

CHOCOLATE CHIP COOKIES
Makes 36

4 oz (110 g) butter
3 oz (75 g) soft light brown sugar
3 oz (75 g) caster sugar
1 egg
a few drops of vanilla essence
6 oz (175 g) plain flour
¼ tsp bicarbonate of soda
pinch of salt
4oz (110 g) cooking chocolate drops or polka dots

Preheat the oven to 375°F/190°C/Gas Mk 5. Cream the butter and sugars together in a bowl until soft. Lightly beat the egg and vanilla essence together and gradually beat into the butter and sugar mixture. Sift together the flour, bicarbonate of soda and salt and add half the quantity to the mixture in the bowl, mixing to a smooth paste. Gradually add the remaining flour mixture and chocolate drops and mix to a firm dough. Place teaspoonfuls of the dough onto greased baking sheets, leaving room for the cookies to spread and cook in the oven for 12 minutes until golden. Cool on the baking sheets for 5 minutes, then transfer to wire racks, using a palette knife. As the cookies cool, they will become crisp.

MUESLI COOKIES
Makes 16

4 oz (110 g) low-fat margarine
4 tbsp granulated sugar
4 oz (110 g) raisins
8 oz (225 g) unsweetened muesli
3 tbsp plain flour
2 oz (50 g) desiccated coconut
2 eggs, beaten

Preheat the oven to 350°F/180°C/Gas Mk 4. Melt the margarine gently in a medium-sized saucepan, cool slightly and then stir in the remaining ingredients. Grease two baking trays and put rounded tablespoonfuls of the mixture about 2 inches (5 cm) apart from each other, flattening the top slightly. Bake in the oven for 12-15 minutes until firm to the touch and golden in colour. Remove from the oven, cool slightly and transfer gently to wire racks to cool

VANILLA BISCUITS
Makes 16

4 oz (110 g) margarine
4 oz (110 g) caster sugar
1 egg yolk
1 tbsp milk
a few drops of vanilla essence
6 oz (175 g) plain flour, sifted
1 tsp baking powder
pinch of salt
2 tbsp cornflour
2 oz (50 g) fine semolina

Beat together the margarine and sugar until the mixture is fluffy. Whisk the egg yolk with the milk and vanilla and add to the creamed margarine. Mix until well blended. Sift the flour, baking powder, salt and cornflour into the mixture, add the semolina, and work thoroughly until a dough is formed. The mixture should then be chilled for 30 minutes as it will be soft. Preheat the oven to 375°F/190°C/ Gas Mk 5. Roll out the dough on a floured surface and cut into small shapes as required. Place on a baking sheet and cook in the oven for about 5 minutes. Leave to cool on the sheet.

CINNAMON COOKIES
Makes 16

4 oz (110 g) butter
2 oz (50 g) granulated sugar
1 egg yolk
5 oz (150 g) self-raising flour, sifted
pinch of salt
1½ tsp ground cinnamon
3 oz (75 g) California raisins
2 oz (50 g) chopped walnuts

Rub butter and sugar together to form a creamy mixture. Beat in egg yolk, then stir sifted flour ,salt and cinnamon into the mixture with the raisins and walnuts. Mix until a firm dough forms. On a lightly floured surface roll into a 2 inch (5 cm) wide 'sausage'. Flatten slightly with rolling pin and then wrap in cling film and refrigerate for at least 1 hour. Preheat the oven to 375°F/190°C/Gas Mk 5. Cut the cookie dough into 1¼ inch (5 mm) slices. Place on lightly greased baking trays and cook for 12-15 minutes until just firm to the touch and golden. Cool slightly, then transfer to wire racks to cool completely.

ALMOND COOKIES
Makes 14

4 oz (110 g) butter
2 oz (50 g) granulated sugar
1 egg yolk
few drops almond essence
pinch of salt
5 oz (150 g) plain flour, sifted
2 oz (50 g) shelled blanched almond slivers

Preheat the oven to 350°F/180°C/Gas Mk 4. Beat together the butter and sugar to form a creamy mixture. Beat in egg yolk, almond essence and salt. Stir sifted flour and almonds into the mixture and knead to a smooth dough. On a lightly floured surface roll into a 2 inch (5 cm) wide 'sausage'. Flatten slightly with rolling pin and then wrap in clingfilm and refrigerate for at least 30 minutes. Cut the cookie dough into ¼ inch (5 mm) slices. Place on lightly greased baking trays. Cook for 12-15 minutes or until just firm to the touch and golden. Cool slightly and transfer to wire racks to cool completely.

KIDS' DELIGHT
Makes 10

4 oz (110 g) butter
2 oz (50 g) granulated sugar
1 egg yolk
5 oz (150 g) plain flour, sifted
pinch of salt
3 tbsp cocoa powder, sifted
3 oz (75 g) California raisins
3 oz (75 g) white chocolate drops

Beat butter and sugar together to form a creamy, thick, pale mixture. Beat in the egg yolk and then stir in the sifted flour, salt and cocoa powder. Stir in raisins and chocolate drops. On a lightly floured surface roll into a 2 inch (5 cm) wide 'sausage'. Flatten slightly with a rolling pin and then wrap in cling film and refrigerate for at least 30 minutes. Preheat the oven to 350°F/180°C/Gas Mk 4. Cut cookie dough into ¼ inch (5 mm) slices, place on lightly greased baking trays and cook for 12-15 minutes or until just firm to the touch and golden. Leave on the baking tray to cool slightly for 5 minutes and then transfer to wire racks to cool completely.

DE LUXE COOKIES
Makes 12

4 oz (110 g) butter
2 oz (50 g) soft brown sugar
2 tbsp condensed milk
1 tbsp water
6 oz (175 g) self-raising flour, sifted
2 oz (50 g) plain chocolate, chopped
1 oz (25 g) white chocolate, chopped
2 oz (50 g) California raisins
1 oz (25 g) dried ready-to-eat apricots, chopped
½ oz (15 g) each of white and plain chocolate, finely grated

Preheat the oven to 350°F/180°C/Gas Mk 4. Beat the butter and sugar together to form a creamy, thick, pale mixture. Beat in the condensed milk and water. Stir in sifted flour, chopped chocolate, raisins and apricots. Divide the mixture into 12 balls, place on lightly greased baking trays and press down lightly with a fork. Cook in the oven for 12-15 minutes or until just firm to the touch and golden. Cool slightly on trays and sprinkle over grated plain and white chocolate whilst cookies are still warm. Transfer to wire racks to cool completely.

PEANUT CRACKERS
Makes 12

1½ oz (40 g) soft brown sugar
2 oz (50 g) granulated sugar
2 oz (50 g) butter
½ beaten egg
a few drops of vanilla essence
4 tbsp crunchy peanut butter
4 oz (110 g) plain flour, sifted

Beat together the sugars and butter. Beat in the egg and vanilla essence, then mix in the peanut butter. Gradually add the flour and mix to a smooth dough. Place small balls of the dough on greased baking sheets, leaving room for them to spread. Score lines on top with a fork. Bake in the oven for 15 minutes until firm. Transfer to a wire rack to cool.

CHERRY ROUNDS
Makes 30

4 oz (110 g) butter, softened
8 oz (225 g) caster sugar
1 egg, beaten
few drops vanilla essence
syrup from Maraschino cherries (see below)
4 oz (110 g) raisins, finely chopped
6 oz (175 g) plain flour, sifted
2 oz (50 g) cocoa powder, sifted
¼ tsp each of salt, baking powder and baking soda
30 Maraschino flavoured cherries, drained (retain syrup)
2 oz (50 g) plain chocolate
1½ tbsp milk

Preheat the oven to 350°F/180°C/Gas Mk 4. Beat butter and sugar until creamy. Add egg, vanilla essence and raisins and mix well. Add sifted dry ingredients and mix well. Stir in enough reserved cherry syrup to make a firm dough. Melt the chocolate with the milk. Divide dough into small balls, place on lightly greased baking trays and press down lightly with a fork. Indent the centre of each biscuit and put a few pieces of chocolate into each hollow. Place a cherry on top and cook in the oven for 10-12 minutes or until just firm to the touch. Cool slightly on trays and then transfer to wire racks to cool completely.

DANISH DELIGHTS
Makes 30

8 oz (225 g) very soft butter
6 oz (175 g) sugar
1 tsp vanilla essence
14 oz (400 g) plain flour, sifted
1 level tsp baking powder
equal quantities of ground cinnamon and icing sugar for dredging

Preheat the oven to 400°F/200°C/Gas Mk 6. Cream butter and sugar together until light and fluffy. Add the vanilla essence. Sift the flour and baking powder together and fold in. Make walnut-sized balls and roll in the cinnamon/sugar mixture. Bake on greased baking sheets for 10 minutes or until they start to brown and the surface starts to crack. Cool completely on a wire rack before storing.

CALIFORNIA CRUNCHIES
Makes 20

2 oz (50 g) golden syrup
5 oz (150 g) butter, softened
4 oz (110 g) demerara sugar
½ oz (15 g) cocoa powder
1 tbsp coffee essence
2 oz (50 g) desiccated coconut
3 oz (75 g) oats
1 oz (25 g) shelled pecan nuts, chopped
2 oz (50 g) raisins
5 oz (150 g) plain flour, sifted
1 egg, beaten

Preheat the oven to 350°F/180°C/Gas Mk 4. Put the syrup, butter sugar, cocoa powder and coffee essence in a large saucepan and heat gently until melted. Remove from heat and stir in coconut, oats, pecan nuts, raisins and flour until well mixed. Cool slightly and then stir in the egg and shape into balls. Flatten slightly and place on lightly greased baking trays. Cook for 15 minutes or until just firm to the touch. Cool slightly on trays and then transfer to wire racks to cool completely.

BRAN BUNDLES
Makes 40

2 oz (50 g) golden syrup
4 tbsp vegetable oil
1 tsp baking soda
2 tsp ground cinnamon
4 oz (110 g) self-raising wholemeal flour
6 oz (175 g) oatbran
2 oz (50 g) plain flour
¼ pt (150 ml) natural yoghurt
¼ pt (150 ml) milk
1 tsp vanilla essence
4 oz (110 g) demerara sugar
4 oz (110 g) raisins

Beat together all the ingredients in a large bowl. Cover and leave overnight in the refrigerator. Preheat oven to 350°F/180°C/Gas Mk 4. Drop tablespoonfuls of the mixture on lightly greased baking trays and flatten slightly. Cook for 10-15 minutes until golden. Cool slightly on trays and then transfer to racks to cool completely.

CHOCOLATE AND RAISIN DROPS
Makes 8

4 oz (110 g) low-fat margarine
2 tsp caster sugar or sweetener
4 oz (110 g) plain wholemeal flour
¼ tsp baking powder
pinch of salt
½ oz (15 g) cocoa or carob powder
few drops vanilla essence
3 oz (75 g) raisins, finely chopped
4 tbsp milk
1 egg white, lightly beaten

Beat the margarine until light and fluffy and then beat in the sugar or sweetener. Sift flour, baking powder, salt and cocoa or carob powder together and fold into the margarine mixture alternately with the vanilla essence, raisins and milk until a firm, soft dough is formed. Spoon the mixture onto greased baking trays and flatten slightly. Brush with beaten egg white and sprinkle with caster sugar or a few flaked or chopped nuts if preferred. Bake for 15 minutes or until just firm. Cool slightly before transferring to a wire rack to cool.

GEORGIAN GINGERBREADS
Makes 24

4 oz (110 g) butter or firm margarine
4 oz (110 g) caster sugar
2 level tsp ground ginger
4 oz (110 g) self-raising flour, sifted

Preheat the oven to 140°C/275°F/Gas Mk 1. Cream the fat and sugar together well. Add the ginger and the flour a little at a time until a stiff dough is formed. Roll into balls about twice the size of a walnut and put on an ungreased baking sheet spaced well apart. Bake for 45 minutes in the lower half of the oven. Remove gently and place on wire cooling racks until completely cold.

RAISIN AND BANANA BAKES
Makes 16

2 ripe bananas
2 oz (50 g) medium oatmeal
1 oz (25 g) sunflower seeds
3 oz (75 g) chopped almonds
3 oz (75 g) raisins
2 oz (50 g) wholemeal self-raising flour
1 oz (25 g) low-fat margarine
3 tbsp clear honey
2 egg yolks, lightly beaten
1 tbsp lemon juice
4 oz (110 g) dried banana slices (optional)

Mash the bananas in a mixing bowl and mix in the oatmeal, sunflower seeds, almonds, raisins and flour. Heat the margarine and honey gently in a saucepan and stir into the oatmeal mixture. Stir in the beaten egg yolks, mix well and arrange tablespoonfuls of the mixture on lightly greased baking trays, flattening the tops slightly. Bake for 15-20 minutes until just firm and golden brown. If desired, a dried banana slice can be placed on top of each cookie at this stage to decorate. Let the cookies cool slightly before placing on wire racks to cool completely.

FUNNY FACE COOKIES
Makes 12

4 oz (110 g) butter or margarine
2½ oz (65 g) granulated sugar
1 egg yolk
pinch of salt
5 oz (150 g) plain flour, sifted
3 oz (75 g) raisins
3 oz (75 g) glacé cherries, chopped
1 oz (25 g) granulated sugar

Beat together the margarine and sugar until thick and creamy. Beat in egg yolk and salt. Stir in sifted flour together with 2 oz (50 g) each of the raisins and cherries. Mix to a firm dough, divide into 12 small balls and coat with the sugar. Place the balls on a light greased baking tray, spaced well apart. Using a flat bottomed glass flatten the cookies and press two raisins for eyes and a piece of cherry for a mouth into each cookie. Bake in the oven for 12-15 minutes until just firm. Cool slightly and transfer to wire racks to cool completely.

GINGER CRISPS
Makes 15

4 oz (110 g) butter or margarine
4 oz (110 g) caster sugar
4 oz (110 g) Muscovado sugar
1 egg, beaten
12 oz (350 g) plain flour, sifted
1 tsp baking powder
1½ tsp ground cinnamon
1 tsp ground ginger
½ tsp ground cloves
½ tsp grated nutmeg
6 oz (175 g) raisins, chopped

Beat together the butter or margarine and the two types of sugar until thick and creamy, then stir in the beaten egg. Sift the flour together with the baking powder and all the spices. Stir into the butter mixture with the raisins and mix to a firm dough. Roll out on a floured board and cut into rounds with a 3 inch (7.5 cm) round fluted cutter. Place on lightly greased baking trays and bake for 15-20 minutes until just firm. Cool slightly and transfer to wire racks to cool completely.

NUTTY HONEY BUNCHES
Makes 18

3 eggs
6 tbsp sunflower oil
6 oz (175 g) clear honey
pinch of salt
½ tsp ground cinnamon
7 oz (200 g) porridge oats
6 oz (175 g) raisins
2 oz (50 g) chopped nuts
3 oz (75 g) chocolate chips
1 oz (25 g) dried skimmed milk powder
2 oz (50 g) bran

In a large bowl mix together the eggs, oil, honey, salt and cinnamon. Stir in the oats, raisins, nuts, chocolate chips, milk powder and bran. Mix well and place rounded tablespoons of dough on lightly greased baking sheets and flatten slightly. Bake for 10-15 minutes until just firm and golden brown. Cool slightly and transfer to wire racks to cool completely.

BOOZY FRUIT AND NUT CLUSTERS
Makes 20

1 lb (450 g) mixed dried fruit, chopped
8 oz (225 g) glacé cherries
8 tbsp sherry or rum
2 oz (50 g) soft butter
4 oz (110 g) soft dark brown sugar
2 eggs, beaten
6 oz (175 g) plain flour, sifted
1½ level tsp bicarbonate of soda
2 level tsp ground cinnamon
½ level tsp ground nutmeg
½ level tsp ground allspice
1 lb (450 g) chopped nuts

Soak the dried fruit and cherries overnight in the sherry or rum. Preheat the oven to 325°F/170°C/Gas Mk 3. Cream together the butter and sugar, then add the eggs and beat until light and fluffy. Stir in sifted flour, soda and spices. Add the chopped nuts and soaked fruit to the mixture. Grease baking sheets and drop teaspoonfuls of mixture, evenly spaced, on to the sheets. Bake for about 15 minutes. (If you do not have many baking sheets, place the clusters on greased foil, and, as a batch finishes cooking, replace with a new batch.) Cool on wire racks.

COCONUT MACAROONS
Makes 24

3 large egg whites
8 oz (225 g) sugar
1 oz (25g) cornflour
5 oz (150g) shredded coconut
1 tsp vanilla essence
1 tsp almond essence

Preheat the oven to 300°F/150°C/Gas Mk 3. Whisk egg whites until thick and shiny. Continue beating adding the sugar a little at a time. Mix the coconut and cornflour together and fold into the egg whites. Cook the mixture gently in a bowl placed over a saucepan of simmering water for about 15 minutes, stirring all the time. Stir in the essences. Drop tablespoonfuls onto a greased baking sheet leaving space between each to allow for spreading. Bake for 25 minutes until light brown. Cool on a rack before putting in a tin. These macaroons dry out quickly, so should be eaten within 2 days.

PEANUT BUTTER COOKIES
Makes 20

8 oz (225 g) soft butter
8 oz (225 g) dark soft brown sugar
8 oz (225 g) caster sugar
2 eggs, beaten
1 tsp vanilla essence
12 oz (350 g) plain flour, sifted
1 level tsp salt
1 level tsp bicarbonate of soda
8 oz (225 g) crunchy peanut butter

Preheat the oven to 400°F/200°C/Gas Mk 6. Cream together the butter and sugars, then add the eggs, and vanilla essence and beat until light and creamy. Beat in the peanut butter. Sift together flour, salt and bicarbonate of soda and fold into the mixture, blending well. Roll balls of dough between your palms and place about 1 inch (2.5 cm) apart on greased baking sheets or greased foil. (If using the foil, as one batch is cooked, remove from baking sheet and replace with another sheet of foil with cookie mixture already on it.) Flatten the cookies slightly and bake for about 8 minutes. Cool on a wire rack.

WALNUT AND CHOCOLATE CHIP COOKIES
Makes 15

8 oz (225 g) soft butter
2 eggs
2 tsp vanilla essence
1 tsp water
8 oz (225 g) dark soft brown sugar
4 oz (110 g) caster sugar
1 lb (450 g) plain flour ,sifted
1 level tsp salt
1 level tsp bicarbonate of soda
12 oz (350 g) chocolate chips
8 oz (225 g) chopped walnuts

Preheat the oven to 375°F/190°C /Gas Mk 5. Beat together butter, eggs and vanilla essence until light and creamy and then add the water. Add both the sugars and mix until well blended. Sift together flour, salt and bicarbonate of soda and fold into the butter mixture. Stir in chocolate chips and walnuts. Drop small quantities onto greased baking sheets, leaving 2 inches (5 cm) between the biscuits. Bake for about 10-12 minutes. Cool on a wire rack.

CHOCOLATE MOUNTAINS
Makes 60

4 oz (110 g) unsweetened cocoa powder
5 fl oz (150 ml) vegetable oil
1 lb (450 g) sugar
2 tsp vanilla essence
4 eggs, beaten
12 oz (350 g) plain flour, sifted
½ level tsp salt
2 level tsp baking powder
icing sugar for dredging

Beat together the cocoa powder, oil, sugar, vanilla essence and eggs until smooth. Sift together the flour, salt and baking powder and fold into chocolate mixture. Blend well and chill overnight in a covered bowl. Preheat the oven to 350°F/175°C/ Gas Mk 4. Shape teaspoonfuls of dough and roll in icing sugar until thoroughly coated. Space cookies at least 1½ inches (4 cm) apart on baking sheets and bake for about 12 minutes, until the surface is crinkled and crisp, while the inside is still soft. Cool on a wire rack.

DIGESTIVES
Makes 30

2 oz (50 g) butter
2 oz (50 g) soft lard
3 tbsp boiling water
1 egg, beaten
4 oz (110 g) plain flour
8 oz (225 g) wholemeal flour
½ level tsp salt
¼ level tsp ground nutmeg
2 oz (50 g) sugar
pinch of allspice

Preheat the oven to 350°F/175°C/Gas Mk 4. Beat together the butter and lard, add the boiling water and beat until soft and fluffy (which is easier with an electric mixer). Stir in the egg. Fold all the dry ingredients into the fat mixture until the dough cleans the bowl. Roll out on a floured board to about ⅛ inch (2 mm) thickness. Prick with a fork and cut into rounds. Bake on greased baking sheets for 25 minutes and cool on a rack.

SPICY CHRISTMAS COOKIES
Makes 60

5 fl oz (150 ml) cold strong black coffee
2 oz (50 g) sugar
13 tbsp molasses
4 oz (110 g) soft butter
juice and rind of 1 lemon
4 oz (110 g) soft dark brown sugar
1 lb (450 g) plain flour, sifted
1 level tsp bicarbonate of soda
1 level tsp ground cinnamon
1 level tsp ground ginger
1 level tsp ground cloves
2 oz (50 g) chopped candied peel
2 oz (50 g) ground almonds

Topping:
1 egg white, lightly beaten
icing sugar

Preheat the oven to 350°F/180°C/Gas Mk 4. Beat the coffee, sugar, molasses, butter, lemon juice and rind and brown sugar until well blended. Sift the dry ingredients together and fold into the sugar mixture. When blended, fold in the peel and ground almonds. Roll teaspoonfuls of the dough between your palms and place (not too far apart) on greased baking sheets. Brush with egg white and bake for 10 minutes or until brown. Cool slightly on a wire rack and, while still warm, roll in icing sugar. Cool completely before storing.

SHREWSBURY BISCUITS
Makes 15

8 oz (225 g) plain flour, sifted
4 oz (110 g) margarine
4 oz (110 g) caster sugar
1 egg, beaten

Sift the flour into a bowl and rub in the margarine until the mixture resembles fine breadcrumbs. Stir in the sugar, add the egg and mix to a very stiff dough. Place on a floured surface, knead quickly and roll out thinly. Cut into round shapes, place on a greased baking sheet and cook in the oven for 12 minutes. Cool on the baking sheet.

GARIBALDI BISCUITS
Makes 18

4 oz (110 g) self-raising flour, sifted
pinch of salt
1 oz (25 g) margarine
2 tbsp milk
2 oz (50 g) currants
1 oz (25 g) caster sugar

Preheat the oven to 375°F/190°C/Gas Mk 5. In a large bowl fork together the flour, salt, margarine and milk, mixing well until smooth. Cut in two equal halves and roll out one piece on a lightly floured board to about ¼ inch (5 mm) thick. Lift onto a lightly greased baking sheet. Sprinkle this pastry with the currants and sugar, leaving half an inch of the pastry uncovered all around the edge. Roll out the second half of pastry to the same size and thickness. Dampen the bare edges of the pastry on the baking sheet and lay the second half on top, sealing the edges. Roll the rolling pin very lightly over the top until the currants are just visible through the pastry. Mark into nine squares, then across diagonally to make eighteen triangles. Brush lightly with wate, sprinkle with sugar and bake for 15 minutes until firm and crisp.

CHERRY AND NUT COOKIES
Makes 25-30

8 oz (225 g) plain flour, sifted
pinch of salt
3 oz (75 g) butter
4 oz (110 g) caster sugar
1 egg, separated
1 tsp lemon rind
milk to mix
4 oz (110 g) chopped nuts of your choice
15 glacé cherries, halved

Preheat the oven to 350°F/180°C/Gas Mk 4. Sift the flour and salt together in a bowl. Rub in the butter until the mixture resembles fine breadcrumbs. Add the sugar, egg yolk and lemon rind and mix to a soft dough with milk. Roll the dough into small balls, dip them in the lightly beaten egg white, then roll in the chopped nuts. Place on greased baking sheets, press half a glacé cherry in the centre of each one and bake for 20-25 minutes. Cool on a wire rack.

NUT COOKIES
Makes 12

2 oz (50 g) butter
1 oz (25 g) caster sugar
3 oz (75 g) flour, sifted
1 oz (25 g) mixed ground nuts

Preheat the oven to 325°F/170°C/Gas Mk 3. Cream the butter and sugar together and stir in the flour and the nuts. Turn onto a floured surface and knead lightly. Roll out thinly between sheets of non-stick paper and cut out 12 rounds about 2 inches (5 cm) in diameter. Arrange on greased baking sheets and cook for 20-25 minutes. Cool on a wire rack.

SAVOURY OATMEAL BISCUITS
Makes 6

1 oz (25 g) margarine
4 oz (110 g) fine oatmeal
a good pinch of salt
water to mix

Preheat the oven to 425°F/220°C/Gas Mk 7. In a bowl rub the margarine into the oatmeal and salt. Add sufficient water to give a dry mixture. Roll out on a floured surface until wafer thin. Cut into round shapes and place on a lightly greased baking sheet. Bake in the oven for 10 minutes until golden.

SUNFLOWER CRISPIES
Makes 20

2 oz (50 g) sunflower seeds
3 oz (75 g) wholemeal flour
1 oz (25 g) ground rice
2 tbsp corn oil
2 tbsp cold water

Preheat the oven to 375°F/190°C/Gas Mk 5. Crush the sunflower seeds with a pestle and mortar (or use a blender). Mix the sunflower seeds, flour and ground rice together. Add the oil and water and work to a dough. Turn out onto a floured surface and roll out. Cut into small shapes and place on a lightly oiled baking sheet. Bake for 12 minutes Leave to cool and crisp on a wire cooling tray.

GRANTHAM GINGERBREADS
Makes 30

4 oz (110 g) butter
12 oz (350 g) caster sugar
1 egg, beaten
9 oz (250 g) self-raising flour, sifted
1 tsp ground ginger

Preheat the oven to 300°F/150°C/Gas Mk 2. Cream the butter and sugar together in a bowl and add the egg. Sift the flour and ginger together and gradually beat into the egg mixture. Roll the dough into small balls and place on greased baking sheets. Bake in oven for 40-45 minutes until crisp, hollow and lightly browned. Cool on wire racks.

ALMOND JUMBLIES
Makes 18

5 oz (150 g) butter
4 oz (110 g) caster sugar
1 egg, beaten
10 oz (300 g) self-raising flour, sifted
pinch of salt
1 level tsp finely grated lemon rind
2 oz (50 g) ground almonds

Preheat the oven to 350°F/180°C/Gas Mk 4. Cream the butter and sugar together and add half the egg. Stir in the flour, salt, lemon rind, almonds and remaining egg. Form the mixture into rolls, shape each into an S and place on a greased baking sheet. Cook for 10 minutes.

SHREWSBURY CURRANT BISCUITS
Makes 16

8 oz (225 g) plain flour, sifted
4 oz (110 g) margarine
4 oz (110 g) caster sugar
2 oz (50 g) currants
1 egg, beaten

Preheat the oven 375°F/190°C/Gas Mk 5. Sift the flour into a bowl and rub in the margarine until the mixture resembles fine bread-crumbs. Stir in the sugar and currants, add the beaten egg and mix to a very stiff dough. Place on a floured surface, knead quickly and roll out thinly. Cut into round shapes, place on a greased baking sheet and cook for 12 minutes. Leave to cool on the baking sheet.

VANILLA SNAPS
Makes 16

8 oz (225 g) butter, softened
8 oz (225 g) caster sugar
2 tsp vanilla essence
½ tsp salt
2 eggs
10 oz (300 g) self-raising flour, sifted

Preheat the oven to 350°F/180°C/Gas Mk 4. Place the butter and sugar in a bowl and cream until light and fluffy. Add the vanilla essence and salt. Beat in the eggs, one at a time. Stir in the flour and mix well. Drop spoonfuls of the mixture on ungreased baking sheets and flatten slightly. Bake in oven for 8-10 minutes until a pale creamy colour. Transfer to wire racks to cool.

CHOCOLATE VIENNESE SLICES
Makes 18

4 oz (110 g) butter
1 oz (25 g) icing sugar, plus a little extra for dredging
4 oz (110 g) flour
1 oz (25 g) plain chocolate, melted
¼ tsp baking powder
1 level tbsp drinking chocolate powder
few drops vanilla essence

Preheat the oven to 375°F/190°C/Gas Mk 5. Beat the butter until smooth and beat in the icing sugar together with the cooled, but still liquid chocolate. Sift in the dry ingredients and beat well. Add a few drops of vanilla essence. Pipe into fingers about 3 inches (7.5 cm) long on greased baking sheets and cook for 15-20 minutes. Cool on a wire rack and dredge with icing sugar before serving.

LEMON AND ORANGE COOKIES
Makes 30

6 oz (175 g) butter
8 oz (225 g) self-raising flour, sifted
pinch of salt
4 oz (110 g) caster or icing sugar, sifted
1 level tsp finely grated lemon and orange rind
1 egg, beaten

Mix together the flour and salt and rub in the butter. Add the sugar and the lemon and orange rind. Mix to a very firm dough with the egg. Knead gently until smooth, then wrap in clingfilm and chill in the refrigerator for 30 minutes. Preheat the oven to 350°F/180°C/ Gas Mk 4. Roll out the dough thinly and cut into rounds about 2 inches (5 cm) in diameter. Place the biscuits on greased baking trays and prick with a fork. Bake for about 12-15 minutes. Cool on a wire rack.

CITRUS BISCUITS
Makes 20

4 oz (110 g) butter or firm margarine
4 oz (110 g) caster sugar
1 tsp lemon or orange rind
1 egg, separated
pinch of salt
6 oz (150 g) plain flour
1 oz (25 g) semolina
extra caster sugar for dredging

Preheat the oven to 350°F/180°C/Gas Mk 4. Cream together the butter, sugar and lemon or orange rind. Beat in the egg yolk and a pinch of salt. Beat in the sifted flour and the semolina until a firm paste is formed. If the mixture is too soft wrap it in greaseproof paper and leave in the refrigerator to firm for 30 minutes. Roll out thinly on a floured board and cut with fluted or shaped cutters. Place on lightly greased baking trays. Whisk the egg white until frothy and brush the tops of the biscuits with it. Dredge with caster sugar and bake near the top of the oven for 12–15 minutes or until lightly golden. Leave on the tray for a few minutes to harden and then remove carefully to a wire cooling rack.

SPECULATIUS
Makes 30

3 oz (75 g) butter
6 oz (175 g) plain flour
1 egg, beaten
3 oz (75 g) brown sugar
pinch cloves
pinch cardamom
1 tsp cinnamon

Preheat the oven to 350°F/180°C/Gas Mk 4. Rub the butter into the flour. Cream the egg with the sugar and add to the flour and butter mixture. Add the spices and mix together gently. Cut into shapes and put on a greased baking tray. Bake in the oven for 10 minutes or until golden brown. Cool and store in an airtight container. The biscuits will keep for several weeks.

DOUBLE CHOCOLATE BISCUITS
Makes 12

3 oz (75 g) margarine
2 oz (50 g) soft brown sugar
2 tsp cocoa powder
few drops vanilla essence
4 oz (110 g) self-raising flour, sifted
1 oz (25 g) cornflakes
pinch of salt
plain chocolate

Preheat the oven to 325°F/170°C/Gas Mk 3. Cream the margarine and sugar together until light and fluffy and stir in the cocoa powder, vanilla essence and salt. Beat well. Beat in the self-raising flour and crushed cornflakes alternately until the mixture is quite stiff. Knead well. Using your hands, shape into walnut-sized balls and place them on a greased baking tray allowing space for them to spread. Flatten each ball slightly with the palm of your hand. Bake for 15 minutes until just firm. Melt the chocolate in a bowl placed over a saucepan of simmering water. When the biscuits are cold, swirl the melted chocolate over the tops and leave to set.

RIBBON BISCUITS
Makes 16

3 eggs, separated
3 oz (75 g) caster sugar
1 tsp vanilla sugar
few drops vanilla essence
3½ oz (90 g) plain flour, sifted

Preheat the oven to 350°F/180°C/Gas Mk 4. Beat the egg yolks and sugar until thick and creamy. The mix should hold a ribbon shape for a few minutes when trailed across the bowl. In another clean bowl whisk the egg whites until stiff and fold into the creamed mixture alternately with the sifted flour and vanilla sugar and essence. Fill into a piping bag with a fluted or plain ½ inch (10 mm) nozzle. Line a baking tray with greaseproof paper and pipe finger-sized lengths of the biscuit mixture onto it. Dust lightly with sifted icing sugar. Bake for 10 minutes or until firm to the touch and golden brown in colour. Remove gently from the greaseproof paper and leave to cool completely on a wire cooling rack.

OAT CRUNCHIES
Makes 16

1 oz (25 g) plain flour, sifted
1 level tsp baking powder
½ level tsp salt
6 oz (175 g) wholemeal flour
1 oz (25 g) medium oatmeal
3 oz (75 g) butter
5 tbsp milk

Preheat the oven to 400°F/200°C/Gas Mk 6. Combine all the dry ingredients and rub in the butter. Mix to a firm dough with the milk. Roll out on a floured work surface until ¼ inch (5 mm) thick. Cut into rounds and place on a greased baking tray. Brush with milk and bake for about 10 minutes, until just golden.

GINGER CRUNCHIES
Makes 8

1 oz (25 g) plain flour, sifted
1 level tsp baking powder
½ level tsp salt
6 oz (175 g) wholemeal flour
½ tsp ground ginger
3 oz (75 g) butter
5 tbsp milk

Preheat the oven to 400°F/200°C/Gas Mk 6. Combine all the dry ingredients and rub in the butter. Mix to a firm dough with the milk. Roll out on a floured work surface until ¼ inch (5 mm) thick. Cut into rounds and place on a greased baking tray. Brush with milk and bake for about 10 minutes, until just golden.

ALMOND CRUNCHIES
Makes 16

1 oz (25 g) plain flour, sifted
1 level tsp baking powder
½ level tsp salt
6 oz (175 g) wholemeal flour
1 oz (25 g) ground almonds
3 oz (75 g) butter
5 tbsp milk

Preheat the oven to 400°F/200°C/Gas Mk 6. Combine all the dry ingredients and rub in the butter. Mix to a firm dough with the milk. Roll out on a floured work surface until ¼ inch (5 mm) thick. Cut into rounds and place on a greased baking tray. Brush with milk and bake for about 10 minutes until just golden.

CORNISH FAIRINGS
Makes 24

4 oz (110 g) flour
pinch of salt
1 level tsp baking powder
1 level tsp bicarbonate of soda
1 level tsp ground ginger
½ level tsp mixed spice
2 oz (50 g) butter
2 oz (50 g) sugar
3 tbsp golden syrup

Preheat the oven to 400°F/200°C/Gas Mk 6. Sift the flour with the salt, baking powder, bicarbonate of soda, ginger and mixed spice. Rub in the butter and then add the sugar. Warm the syrup and add it to the other ingredients. Mix well to a fairly stiff consistency. Roll into small balls and place them 3 inches (7.5 cm) apart on two greased baking sheets. Bake for about 8 minutes.

CHOCOLATE RING BISCUITS
Makes 25

8 oz (225 g) butter
4 oz (110 g) caster sugar
12 oz (350 g) plain flour, sifted
2 oz (50 g) cocoa powder
pinch of salt
6 tbsp apricot or raspberry jam
icing sugar, for dredging

Preheat the oven to 400°F/200°C/Gas Mk 6. Place the butter and sugar in a bowl and cream together until light and fluffy. Add the flour, cocoa powder and salt, and work the mixture to make a firm dough. Roll out on a lightly floured surface and cut into 2 inch (5 cm) rounds with a plain cutter. Cut out the centres of half the biscuits using a 1 inch (2.5 cm) cutter. Place all the biscuits on greased baking sheets and bake in the oven for 10 minutes Lift out carefully onto a wire rack to cool. Spread the jam on the whole biscuits, piling it higher in the centre, then press on the biscuit rings and sprinkle with the icing sugar.

BOSWORTH JUMBLES
Makes 24

5 oz (150 g) unsalted butter
5 oz (150 g) caster sugar
1 egg
10 oz (300 g) plain flour, sifted
2 oz (50 g) ground almonds
1 tsp grated lemon rind
pinch of ground ginger

Preheat the oven to 350°F/180°C/Gas Mk 4. Cream the butter and sugar together until light and fluffy. Work in the egg with a little of the flour. Add the remaining flour, almonds, lemon rind and ginger to make a soft but firm dough. On a lightly floured surface, roll out the dough out into sausage-shaped pieces about the thickness of a finger. Cut into pieces 5 inches (12.5 cm) long and place on two greased baking sheets curving the biscuits into S shapes. Bake in the oven for 12 minutes. Lift out carefully and place on wire racks to cool.

HONEY FLAPJACKS
Makes 12

5 oz (150 g) butter or hard margarine
3 oz (75 g) light soft brown sugar
2 tbsp clear honey
8 oz (225 g) porridge oats
½ tsp ground ginger

Preheat the oven to 350°F/180°C/Gas Mk 4. Place the butter or margarine in a saucepan and heat until just melted. Stir in the sugar, honey, porridge oats and ginger, mixing thoroughly. Grease a 7 inch (17.5 cm) square shallow tin and press in the mixture. Bake for 25 minutes. While still hot, use a knife to mark into fingers. Leave in the tin until cold, then cut into fingers and lift out.

PEANUT OATIES
Makes 40

4 oz (110 g) butter, softened
4 oz (110 g) crunchy peanut butter
8 oz (225 g) granulated sugar
6 oz (175 g) brown sugar
2 eggs, beaten
4 tbsp milk
1 tsp vanilla essence
7 oz (200 g) self-raising flour, sifted
½ tsp salt
9 oz (250 g) rolled oats
3 oz (75 g) raisins
2 oz (50 g) unsalted peanuts, chopped

Preheat the oven to 350°F/180°C/Gas Mk 4. Place the butter, peanut butter and sugars in a bowl and beat well until creamy. Add the eggs, milk and vanilla essence and beat until well mixed. Gradually stir in the flour and salt, followed by the oats, raisins and peanuts. Arrange spoonfuls of the mixture on ungreased baking sheets, leaving room for the biscuits to spread. Bake for 15 minutes until golden. Transfer to wire racks to cool.

GINGER NUTS
Makes 24

4 oz (110 g) self-raising flour, sifted
½ tsp bicarbonate of soda
2 level tsp ground ginger
1 level tsp ground cinnamon
2 tsp caster sugar
2 oz (50 g) butter
3 oz (75 g) golden syrup

Preheat the oven to 375°F/190°C/Gas Mk 5. Sift the flour, bicarbonate of soda, ginger and cinnamon into a bowl. Add the sugar. Melt the butter and stir in the syrup. Add to the flour mixture and mix well. Divide the mixture into small balls, place well apart on two greased baking sheets and flatten slightly. Bake for 15-20 minutes. Remove from the oven and leave to cool for a few minutes before cooling completely on wire racks.

OATY BISCUITS
Makes 15

3 oz (75 g) plain flour, sifted
½ tsp bicarbonate of soda
3 oz (75 g) caster sugar
3 oz (75 g) rolled oats
3 oz (75 g) butter
1 tbsp milk
1 tbsp golden syrup

Preheat the oven to 300°F/150°C/Gas Mk 2. Sift together the flour and bicarbonate of soda and stir in the sugar and oats. Heat the butter, milk and syrup together until melted, pour into the flour mixture and mix well. Roll into small balls and place on greased baking trays, spaced wide apart. Flatten slightly, then bake in oven for 40 minutes.

TREACLE BISCUITS
Makes 8

3 oz (75 g) soft margarine
3 oz (75 g) light brown sugar
1½ oz (40 g) black treacle
6 oz (175 g) porridge oats
½ tsp ground ginger

Preheat the oven to 375°F/190°C/Gas Mk 5. Melt the margarine in a saucepan, then add the sugar and treacle. Remove from the heat and stir in the porridge oats and the ginger. Mix well and press into a greased 7 inch (17.5 cm) round sandwich tin lined with greaseproof paper. Bake in oven for 20-25 minutes until just firm. Remove and mark into eight pieces. Cool in the tin before turning out and cutting.

CHOCOLATE CRISPIES
Makes 16–20

4 oz (110 g) plain chocolate
½ oz (15 g) butter
2–3 oz (50–75 g) cornflakes

Melt the chocolate and butter in a bowl over a saucepan of hot water. Stir until melted, remove from heat and mix in the cornflakes. Stir well until all the flakes are coated. Place large spoonfuls of the mixture onto greaseproof paper or greaseproof cake papers and leave to set.

ORANGE AND GINGER COOKIES
Makes 27 fingers

4 tbsp treacle
2 eggs, beaten
2 oz (50 g) candied orange peel, chopped
2 oz (50 g) stem ginger, chopped
grated rind and juice of 1 orange
4 oz (110 g) caster sugar
12 oz (350 g) plain flour, sifted
pinch of salt
1 tsp bicarbonate of soda
1 tsp ground cinnamon
2 tsp ground ginger
4 oz (110 g) butter

Preheat the oven to 325°F/170°C/Gas Mk 3. Line a 9 inch (23 cm) square cake tin with foil. In a small saucepan, heat the treacle and stir in the eggs, peel, stem ginger, orange rind and juice and sugar. In a bowl, sift together the flour, salt, bicarbonate of soda, cinnamon and ginger and then rub in the butter. Stir in the treacle mixture and mix well to a pouring consistency. Turn the cookie mixture into the tin, flattening the top. Bake in the oven for 1–1¼ hours. Cut into fingers when cool.

OAT AND ALMOND BISCUITS
Makes 45

4 oz (110 g) soft margarine
3 oz (75 g) light brown sugar
4 oz (110 g) self-raising flour, sifted
4 oz (110 g) porridge oats
1 tbsp clear honey
1 egg, beaten
2 oz (50 g) flaked almonds

Preheat the oven to 350°F/180°C/Gas Mk 4. Mix the margarine, sugar, flour, porridge oats and honey in a bowl and bind with the egg. Lightly grease two baking sheets and place teaspoonfuls of the mixture on the sheets leaving room for them to spread. Top each mixture with one almond and bake for 15 minutes until golden. Leave to cool slightly on the baking sheets before transferring to wire racks to cool completely.

CINNAMON CRISPIES
Makes 28

8 oz (225 g) soft margarine
8 oz (225 g) demerara sugar
8 oz (225 g) self-raising flour, sifted
½ tsp mixed spice
2 tsp ground cinnamon
1 egg, beaten

Preheat the oven to 400°F/200°C/Gas Mk 6. In a bowl mix together the margarine, sugar, flour, mixed spice and cinnamon. Add the beaten egg and blend well. Drop teaspoonfuls of the mixture onto lightly greased baking sheets, leaving room for the biscuits to spread. Bake for 12 minutes until golden brown. Remove from oven and leave to cool on the sheets for a short time, then transfer to wire racks.

CHOCOLATE BISCUITS
Makes 36

4 oz (110 g) margarine
2 oz (50 g) caster sugar
4 oz (110 g) self-raising flour, sifted
1 oz (25 g) cocoa powder

Preheat the oven to 375°F/190°C/Gas Mk 5. Cream together the margarine and sugar in a bowl. Work in the sifted cocoa powder and flour until well blended. Roll the dough into small balls (1 teaspoonful each) and arrange on two large, lightly greased baking sheets. Flatten the tops and bake in the oven for 10 minutes Remove from the oven and leave to cool for a few minutes before transferring to wire racks.

CARAWAY COOKIES
Makes 30

6 oz (175 g) butter
8 oz (225 g) flour
1½ oz (40 g) caster sugar
1 level tsp caraway seeds

Rub the butter into the flour until it starts to bind together. Press into a shallow base-lined Swiss roll tin. Dredge liberally with the caster sugar mixed with the caraway seeds. Leave overnight in the refrigerator. Preheat the oven to 350°F/180°C/Gas Mk 4 and bake for about 20 minutes. Cut into fingers and cool in the tin. Allow to stand for a day before eating.

VANILLA BUTTER BISCUITS
Makes 24

4 oz (110 g) butter
4 oz (110 g) caster sugar
5 oz (150 g) self-raising flour, sifted
2 drops of vanilla essence
12 walnuts, chopped
1 egg, beaten

Preheat the oven to 350°F/180°C/Gas Mk 4. Melt the butter in a small saucepan and boil gently for 3 minutes until golden brown. Remove from the heat and cool. In a bowl mix the sugar, flour, vanilla essence, walnuts and egg. Add the butter and mix until thoroughly blended. Drop teaspoonfuls of the mixture onto lightly greased baking sheets, leaving room for the biscuits to spread. Bake for 15 minutes until dark brown. Remove from the baking sheets and place on wire racks to cool.

BUTTERNUT WAFERS
Makes 20

4 oz (110 g) butter, softened
6 oz (175 g) brown sugar
1 tsp vanilla essence
1 egg
3 oz (75 g) plain flour
1 tsp baking powder
½ tsp salt
2 oz (50 g) finely chopped mixed nuts

Preheat the oven to 400°F/200°C/Gas Mk 6. Place the butter and sugar in a bowl and cream well. Mix in the vanilla essence and beat in the egg until fluffy. Gradually sift in the flour, baking powder and salt, then add the nuts and mix well. Drop spoonfuls of the mixture onto ungreased baking sheets, leaving room for the biscuits to spread. Bake for 5 minutes until crisp and golden. Leave to cool on the sheets for about 30 seconds, then transfer to a wire rack.

WALNUT SPICE FINGERS
Makes 16

6 oz (175 g) soft margarine
8 oz (225 g) light brown sugar
8oz (225 g) self-raising flour, sifted
1 tsp mixed spice
2 oz (50 g) walnuts, chopped

Preheat the oven to 350°F/180°C/Gas Mk 4. In a bowl cream the margarine and sugar until fluffy. Gradually add the flour, mixed spice and walnuts and mix thoroughly. Spread the mixture evenly in a lightly greased Swiss roll tin. Bake for 25 minutes. Remove from the heat and lightly mark the top into sixteen finger shapes. Leave to cool before cutting.

GERMAN BISCUITS
Makes 10

2½ oz (65 g) butter
1¼ oz (40 g) caster sugar
1 egg yolk
3½ oz (90 g) flour
vanilla essence

Preheat the oven to 325°F/170°C/Gas Mk 3. Cream the butter and sugar together in a bowl until white and fluffy. Beat in the egg yolk and add vanilla essence to taste. Sift in the flour and work gently to make a soft dough. Roll out thinly and cut into fancy shapes. Bake on a lightly oiled baking sheet until pale golden in colour.

COCONUT AND CHERRY BISCUITS
Makes 32

4 oz (110 g) soft margarine
4 oz (110 g) caster sugar
1 egg, beaten
8 oz (225 g) self-raising flour, sifted
a little milk
3 oz (75 g) desiccated coconut
8 glacé cherries, cut into quarters

Preheat the oven to 350°F/180°C/Gas Mk 4. Place the margarine, sugar, egg and flour in a bowl and mix well. Place the dough on a floured surface and knead until smooth. Roll out to a thickness of ⅛ inch (3 mm) and use a cutter to cut into rounds of about 2 inches (5 cm). Brush the tops with milk and sprinkle with coconut. Top each with a glacé cherry quarter. Place on lightly greased baking sheets and bake in the oven for 15 minutes until just beginning to colour. Turn out onto wire racks to cool.

LEMON CURD CRUNCHIES
Makes 10

4 oz (110 g) butter
2 oz (50 g) caster sugar
5 oz (150g) plain flour, sifted
lemon curd for filling

Preheat the oven to 350°F/180°C/Gas Mk 4. Place the butter, sugar and flour in a mixing bowl. Mix together and beat well with a wooden spoon until soft and creamy. Spread the mixture evenly in a Swiss roll tin and score lines on the top with a fork. Bake in the oven for 20-25 minutes. Cut into finger shapes and place on a wire rack to cool. When the biscuits are cold, sandwich them together with lemon curd.

ICED GINGER OATIES
Makes 28

4 oz (110 g) margarine
2 level tbsp golden syrup
8 oz (225 g) porridge oats
2 level tsp ground ginger
4 oz (110 g) soft brown sugar

Topping:
6 level tbsp icing sugar, sifted
3 oz (75 g) butter
1 level tsp ground ginger
3 level tsp golden syrup

Preheat the oven to 350°F/180°C/Gas Mk 4. Brush a 7 inch (18 cm) square tin thoroughly with melted margarine. Melt the margarine and syrup together in a saucepan over a gentle heat, and, when melted, remove from the heat and stir in the oats, ginger and sugar. Pack into the prepared tin, levelling the surface. Bake for 20-25 minutes. Put the topping ingredients into a pan and stir over a gentle heat until melted. Pour over the cooked oatcake while it is still warm. Leave to cool slightly and then mark into squares. Remove from the tin while still slightly warm and leave to cool completely before cutting.

CREAM CRACKERS
Makes 10

8 oz (225 g) flour, sifted
½ tsp salt
1–1½ oz (25–40g) fat
water for mixing

Preheat the oven to 450°F/230°C/Gas Mk 8. Sift the flour and salt into a mixing bowl, rub in the fat and, using as little water as possible, gradually mix to a very dry dough. Roll out very thinly on a floured surface. Fold into three, roll again very lightly and cut into squares. Place on greased baking trays and bake in the oven for 7–8 minutes Leave to cool on the baking trays.

CHEESE STRAWS
Makes 80

4 oz (110 g) self-raising flour, sifted
4 oz (110 g) wholemeal flour
salt and pepper
4 oz (110 g) margarine
4 oz (110 g) mature Cheddar cheese, grated
1 egg, beaten

Preheat the oven to 400°F/200°C/Gas Mk 6. Sift the flours into a bowl, and add salt and pepper to taste. Rub in the margarine until the mixture resembles fine breadcrumbs. Mix in the cheese and add sufficient egg to bind to a firm dough. Knead well on a floured surface. Roll out to ¼ inch (5 mm) thickness and cut into narrow fingers. Place on lightly greased baking trays and bake for 10 minutes until just beginning to colour. Leave on the trays for a few minutes then transfer to wire rack to cool.

WHITE BUTTONS
Makes 30

4 oz (110 g) butter
12 oz (350 g) caster sugar
1 egg, beaten
9 oz (250 g) self-raising flour, sifted
1 level tsp ground ginger

Preheat the oven to 300°F/150°C/Gas Mk 2. Beat the butter and sugar together in a bowl until white and fluffy, and then gradually beat in the egg. Sift in the flour and ginger, a little at a time, and work with a fork until the dough is fairly firm. Roll the dough into small, walnut-sized balls and put them on lightly greased baking sheets, spacing them well apart to allow for spreading. Bake for about 40 minutes or until they are crisp, well risen and a pale golden colour. Remove them from the baking sheets and gently roll in caster sugar. Place on wire racks to cool.

COFFEE CRESCENTS
Makes 10

2 oz (50 g) butter
2 oz (50 g) caster sugar
½ beaten egg
1 tsp coffee essence (or to taste)
4 oz (110 g) plain flour
pinch of salt
½ oz nuts, chopped

Preheat the oven to 325°F/170°C/Gas Mk 3. Cream the butter and caster sugar together in a bowl until white and fluffy. Beat in the egg and the coffee essence. Gradually add the sifted flour and salt, gently mixing in, and finally stir in the chopped nuts. Knead lightly and turn out onto a floured board. Roll out thinly and cut into crescent shapes. Place on a lightly greased baking tray and cook for 15 minutes. Remove to a wire rack to cool. If desired, at this stage, one end of each crescent may be dipped in coffee glacé icing and left to set.

MARBLE BISCUITS
Makes 10–12

2 oz (50 g) butter
2 oz (50 g) caster sugar
½ beaten egg
few drops vanilla essence
4 oz (110 g) plain flour
pinch of salt
1 tsp cocoa powder

Preheat the oven to 325°F/170°C/Gas Mk 3. Beat the butter and caster sugar in a bowl until white and fluffy, then beat in the egg. Add vanilla essence to taste. Sift the flour and salt into the mixture and gently fold in. Halve the mixture, add the cocoa powder to one half and mix well. Gently knead the two doughs together and then roll out thinly. Cut into rounds, place on a greased baking tray and bake in the oven for 15 minutes. Remove to a wire rack to cool.

COCONUT BISCUITS
Makes 30

8 oz (225 g) plain flour, sifted
1 tsp baking powder
pinch of salt
4 oz (110 g) butter
4 oz (110 g) caster sugar
4 oz (110 g) desiccated coconut
1 egg, beaten
2 tbsp milk

Preheat the oven to 350°F/180°C/Gas Mk 4. Sift the flour, baking powder and salt together and rub in the butter. Stir in the sugar and desiccated coconut. Bind to a dough with the beaten egg and milk. Knead gently on a lightly floured board. Roll out to ¼ inch (5 mm) thick and cut into 2 inch (5 cm) rounds. Place on lightly greased baking trays and bake in the oven for 15 minutes.

JAM SANDWICH BISCUITS
Makes 30

2 oz (50 g) self-raising flour
2 oz (50 g) cornflour
pinch of salt
4 oz (110 g) butter
2 tbsp icing sugar
few drops vanilla essence

Filling: 1 oz (25 g) butter, softened
3 tbsp icing sugar
few drops vanilla essence
raspberry or strawberry jam

Preheat the oven to 350°F/180°C/Gas Mk 4. Sift the flour, cornflour and salt into a bowl. In another bowl cream together the butter and icing sugar until fluffy. Add vanilla essence to taste. Add half the quantity of the flour to the butter mixture and mix well. Gradually add the remaining flour mixture and beat well to a smooth dough. Place spoonfuls of the dough on greased baking sheets and flatten each one slightly. Bake in the oven for 15–20 minutes until a pale golden colour. Leave to cool. To make the filling, mix the butter, icing sugar and vanilla essence together in a bowl. When the biscuits are cold, spread with the filling and the jam, then sandwich together.

EASTER BISCUITS
Makes 30

8 oz (225 g) plain flour
pinch of salt
½ tsp baking powder
pinch mixed spice
4 oz (110 g) butter
4 oz (110 g) caster sugar
grated rind of ½ lemon
2 oz (50 g) currants
1 egg, beaten

Preheat the oven to 350°F/180°C/Gas Mk 4. Sift together the flour, baking powder, salt and mixed spice in a bowl. Rub in the butter until the mixture resembles fine breadcrumbs. Add the sugar, grated lemon rind and currants and bind with the beaten egg. Knead lightly on a floured board and roll out to ¼ inch (5 mm) thick. Cut into rounds with a 2 inch (5 cm) fluted cutter and place on a greased baking tray. Bake for 15 minutes.

CRACKNELL BISCUITS
Makes 10–12

6 oz (175 g) plain flour, sifted
pinch of salt
2 oz (50 g) cornflour
3 oz (75 g) butter
1 tbsp milk and 1 tbsp water, mixed

Preheat the oven to 350°F/180°C/Gas Mk 4. Sift the plain flour, salt and cornflour into a bowl and rub in the butter until the mixture resembles fine breadcrumbs. Add just enough milk and water to make a very dry dough. Knead well to bind all the ingredients together. Shape into small rounds and place on a lightly greased baking sheet. Using the back of a spoon, press down lightly in the middle of each biscuit. Bake for 12-15 minutes.

SPRINGERLE
Makes 24

1 oz (25 g) butter, melted
3 oz (75 g) aniseed
2 eggs, beaten
10 oz (300 g) caster sugar
1 tsp finely grated lemon rind
few drops vanilla essence
12 oz (350 g) plain flour

Grease baking trays with the melted butter and sprinkle with aniseed. Add the beaten eggs to the sugar and whisk until thick. Beat in the lemon rind and vanilla essence. Add the flour one-third at a time until the mixture forms a soft ball. Knead for 10 minutes. Roll out to ¼ inch (5 mm) thick. Cut into shapes and put on the prepared baking trays. Set aside for 24 hours. Preheat the oven to 250°F/130°C/Gas Mk ½. Bake in the oven for 20–30 minutes or until firm but not brown. Cool and leave uncovered for 2–3 days to soften. Then store in an airtight container. These biscuits will keep for several weeks.

COCONUT SHORTBREAD
Makes 6–8 wedges

3 oz (75 g) butter
1½–2 oz (40-50 g) caster sugar
3 oz (75 g) plain flour
2 tbsp ground rice
2 oz (50 g) desiccated coconut

Preheat the oven to 350°F/180°C/Gas Mk 4. In a mixing bowl, cream the butter and half the amount of sugar until light and then work in the sifted flour, rice and coconut. Work in the remaining sugar. Knead thoroughly and press flat onto an ungreased baking sheet in a circular shape. Using a knife, mark out the top in sections. Bake for 45 minutes and leave to cool on the baking sheet before cutting.

HUNGARIAN BISCUITS
Makes 12

2 oz (50 g) margarine
2 oz (50 g) caster sugar
few drops almond essence
2 oz (50 g) self-raising flour
2 oz (50 g) ground almonds
a few blanched almonds

Preheat the oven to 375°F/190°C/Gas Mk 5. Cream together the margarine and sugar in a bowl. Add almond essence to taste. Stir in the flour and ground almonds and knead well. Roll out thinly on a floured surface, cut into fingers or rounds and place on a lightly greased baking sheet. Place half an almond in the centre of each biscuit and bake in the oven for 10 minutes. Leave to cool on the baking sheet.

CINNAMON LEMON BISCUITS
Makes 14

2 oz (50 g) lard
2 oz (50 g) caster sugar
1 tbsp golden syrup
6 oz (175 g) plain flour, sifted
½ tsp cinnamon
2 tsp finely grated rind of lemon
2 tsp fresh lemon juice

Preheat the oven to 350°F/180°C/Gas Mk 4. Cream the lard, sugar and syrup together in a bowl. Add the flour, cinnamon, lemon rind and juice and mix thoroughly. Knead well, then roll out very thinly on a floured surface and cut into rounds. Place on greased baking sheets and bake for 10 minutes. Cool on the baking sheets.

LEMON AND LIME COOKIES
Makes 24

4 oz (110 g) butter
4 oz (110 g) caster sugar
1 egg yolk
2 oz (50 g) full-fat soft cheese
6 oz (175 g) plain flour, sifted
finely grated rind of 1 small lemon
1 tbsp lemon juice
4 tsp lime marmalade

Preheat the oven to 375°F/190°C/Gas Mk 5. Cream the butter and sugar together in a bowl. Add the egg yolk, cheese, flour, lemon rind and juice and beat well. Spoon small amounts of the mixture onto greased baking sheets, leaving room for the biscuits to spread. Bake for 18 minutes until light brown and transfer to a wire rack to cool. Melt the marmalade in a small saucepan, then brush it over each cookie. Leave to set.

MIDAS MACAROONS
Makes 18

2 oz (50 g) ground almonds
2 oz (50 g) cake crumbs
2 oz (50 g) ground rice
6 oz (175 g) caster sugar
2 large egg whites
few drops almond essence
flaked almonds
rice paper

Preheat the oven to 350°F/180°C/Gas Mk 4. Put the ground almonds, cake crumbs, ground rice and caster sugar into a mixing bowl and stir together until well blended. Whisk the egg whites a little until they are slightly frothy, then stir them into the dry mixture, adding almond essence to taste. Put the rice paper on baking trays, divide the mixture into eighteen pieces and roll each one into a ball about the size of a walnut. Place the macaroons on the baking trays, leaving room for them to spread. Press an almond flake onto each macaroon and flatten them slightly. Bake on the centre shelf of the oven for 15–20 minutes or until they are pale brown in colour. Remove from the baking trays, cut off any excess rice paper and leave to cool.

SHORTBREAD
Makes 6–8 wedges

6 oz (175 g) plain flour, sifted
4 oz (110 g) butter, softened
2 oz (50 g) caster sugar

Preheat the oven to 325°F/170°C/Gas Mk 3. Mix the sifted flour and the sugar together in a bowl. Make a well in the flour and put the softened butter in the centre. Work the flour mix into the butter with your fingers until a smooth round ball is obtained. Press into a short-bread mould or small, round sandwich tin and bake in the centre of the oven for 30–40 minutes or until a pale golden colour. Remove from the oven and sprinkle with caster sugar. Cut with a sharp knife while warm and leave in the tin until cool. Then remove and leave to cool completely on a wire rack.

FREDA'S MACAROONS
Makes 30

rice paper
3 egg whites
10 oz (300 g) caster sugar
8 oz (225 g) ground almonds
few drops almond essence
icing sugar for dusting

Preheat the oven to 350°F/180°C/Gas Mk 4. Line baking sheets with rice paper. Put the egg whites in a bowl and froth up lightly with a fork. Gradually add the sugar, ground almonds and almond essence and mix to a thick paste. Drop teaspoonfuls of the mixture onto the rice paper on the baking sheets, leaving enough space between each for the macaroons to spread. Cook for about 20 minutes, or until the macaroons are pale golden and the tops are cracked. Transfer to a wire rack to cool. Trim away excess rice paper from the bases of the macaroons and dust with icing sugar.

CRUNCHY FINGERS
Makes 20

6 oz (175 g) butter
2 oz (50 g) demerara sugar
6 oz (175 g) golden syrup
6 oz (175 g) rolled oats
1 tsp ground ginger
pinch of salt

Preheat the oven to 325°F/170°C/Gas Mk 3. Melt together the butter, sugar and syrup. When the sugar has dissolved stir in the oats, salt and ground ginger and mix well. Press into a greased Swiss roll tin and bake for about 30 minutes. Cut into fingers in the tray while still warm and then leave to cool.

ABERNETHY BISCUITS
Makes 12

2 oz (50 g) caster sugar
3 tbsp milk
8 oz (225 g) self-raising flour, sifted
pinch of salt
3 oz (75 g) margarine
2 oz (50 g) lard

Preheat the oven to 375°F/190°C/Gas Mk 5. Dissolve the sugar in the milk over a low heat and then leave to cool. Sift the flour and salt into a bowl. Rub in the fats until the mixture resembles fine breadcrumbs, then bind with the sugared milk. Roll out to ¼ inch (5 mm) thick on a lightly floured board and cut into round biscuits. Place on greased baking trays, prick lightly with a fork and bake near the top of the oven for 15 minutes, or until the biscuits are golden. Cool on a wire rack.

CURRIED CHEESE BISCUITS
Makes 20

8 oz (225 g) wholewheat flour
2 level tsp curry powder
pinch of salt and pepper
6 oz (175 g) margarine
4 oz (110 g) Cheddar cheese, finely grated
2 egg yolks

Preheat the oven to 375°F/190°C/Gas Mk 5. Mix together the flour, curry powder, salt and pepper. Rub in the margarine until the mixture resembles fine breadcrumbs. Stir in the grated cheese and mix. Bind to a stiff dough with the egg yolks. Roll out to ¼ inch (5 mm) thick on a floured board. Cut out small rounds with a biscuit cutter and place on a lightly greased baking sheet. Bake for 20 minutes until golden brown. Leave on the baking sheet for 1 minute and then slide off onto a wire rack to cool.

CHEESE CRACKERS
Makes 20

8 oz (225 g) self-raising flour, sifted
½ tsp salt
3 oz (75 g) margarine
about 5 tbsp water
3 oz (75 g) Cheddar cheese, finely grated

Preheat the oven to 375°F/190°C/Gas Mk 5. Sift the flour into a bowl, add the salt and then rub the margarine into the flour until the mixture resembles fine breadcrumbs. Stir in enough water to bind the mixture into a pliable dough. Leave to rest for 5 minutes. Roll out on a floured board to an oblong shape and sprinkle 1 oz (25 g) of the cheese over the lower two-thirds of the pastry. Fold down the top third, then fold down again. Turn once to the left. Roll out again and sprinkle over cheese as before. Fold and turn twice more. Divide the dough into two pieces. Roll out thinly to ¼ inch (5 mm) thick and prick all over with a fork. Cut into squares and place on a lightly greased baking tray. Cook for about 15 minutes.

SHORTIE DIGESTIVE BISCUITS
Makes 12

1 oz (25 g) plain flour
6 oz (175 g) wholemeal flour
1 tsp baking powder
½ tsp salt
3 oz (75 g) butter
1 oz (25 g) oatmeal
sugar to taste
milk to bind

Preheat the oven to 180°C/350°F/Gas Mk 4. Sift the flours, baking powder and salt together in a bowl and rub in the butter until the mixture resembles fine breadcrumbs. Stir in the sugar and oatmeal, mix well, then add just enough milk to bind. Knead the dough lightly, roll out thinly and cut into rounds. Prick all over with a fork and bake on a lightly oiled baking tray for about 20–25 minutes. Do not overbake.

DUTCH KISSES
Makes 18

2 oz (50 g) butter
2 oz (50 g) caster sugar
1 egg yolk
grated rind of ½ lemon
2 oz (50 g) plain flour
pinch of salt
2 level tsp ground ginger
9 walnuts, halved

Preheat the oven to 180°C/350°F/Gas Mk 4. Cream together the butter and sugar until light and fluffy, then beat in the egg yolk and grated lemon rind. Sift in the flour, salt and ginger and mix well. Roll the dough into eighteen small balls between floured palms. Place on greased baking trays, leaving room for the biscuits to spread. Flatten each ball a little, press half a walnut on top of each and bake for 15 minutes.

LEMON SHORTBREAD
Makes 12

4 oz (110 g) butter, softened
2 oz (50 g) caster sugar
4 oz (110 g) plain flour
2 oz (50 g) cornflour
grated rind of 1 large lemon
caster sugar, for sprinkling

Preheat the oven to 325°F/170°C/Gas Mk 3. Cream the butter and sugar in a mixing bowl until light and fluffy. Add the sifted flours and then the lemon rind. Knead until smooth. Press the dough into a lightly greased 7 inch (17.5 cm) square tin and level the top. Bake in the oven for 35 minutes until golden brown. Remove from the oven, lightly mark out the top into twelve finger shapes and leave to cool completely. Turn out onto a wire rack, sprinkle with sugar and cut into the twelve fingers.

ITALIAN CRISP MACAROONS
Makes 24

4 oz (110 g) ground almonds
6 oz (175 g) caster sugar
2 large egg whites
¼ tsp almond essence
icing sugar for dredging

Preheat the oven to 350°F/180°C/Gas Mk 4. Beat the ground almonds, caster sugar and half the egg whites together until thick and creamy. Whisk the remaining egg whites until very stiff and then fold these into the mixture, together with the almond essence. It will form quite a thick paste. Gently roll rounded teaspoonfuls of the dough between your palms and place on non-stick paper on a baking sheet. Bake for about 30 minutes until the macaroons are golden brown and puffed up. Cool on wire trays and dredge with icing sugar.

ICED RAISIN COOKIES
Makes 25

4 oz (110 g) butter
6 oz (175 g) soft brown sugar
1 egg, beaten
8 oz (225 g) plain flour
2 tsp baking powder
1 tsp ground cinnamon

1 tsp mixed spice
pinch salt
4 tbsp soured cream
2 tbsp milk
4 oz (110 g) raisins

Glaze:
4 oz (110 g) icing sugar
3 tbsp boiling water
½ tsp vanilla essence

Preheat the oven to 180°C/350°F/Gas Mark 4. Cream the butter and brown sugar together until light and fluffy. Add the egg a little at a time, beating well after each addition. Sift the flour, baking powder, ground cinnamon, mixed spice and salt together, then fold into the creamed mixture alternately with the soured cream, milk and raisins. Drop tablespoonfuls onto a greased baking sheet, leaving plenty of space in between, as they will spread during cooking, and bake in the oven for about 15 minutes or until brown. Remove from the oven but do not remove from the baking tray. To make the glaze, sift the icing sugar into a bowl and stir in the boiling water and vanilla essence. Brush over the cookies and return to the oven for a further 5 minutes. Remove from the oven and leave to cool on a wire rack.

HAZELNUT SQUARES

2 lb (900 g) demerara sugar
½ pint (300 ml) water
1 tsp vanilla essence
3 oz (75 g) hazelnuts, chopped

Place the sugar and water in a heavy-based saucepan and heat quickly until the sugar has dissolved. Bring to the boil until a drop of the mixture placed in cold water forms a soft ball when rolled with the fingers. Stir in the vanilla essence and nuts and continue boiling. Remove from the heat, leave to cool a little, then beat well. Pour into a buttered shallow square tin and leave to cool. When nearly set, cut into pieces.

SHELL BISCUITS
Makes 12–14

3 oz (75 g) butter
3 oz (75 g) caster sugar
1 small egg, beaten
5 oz (150 g) plain flour
jam for filling
icing sugar for dusting

Preheat the oven to 400°F/200°C/Gas Mk 6. Cream the butter and sugar until light and fluffy. Beat in the egg, fold in the flour and mix well. Place the mixture in a piping bag fitted with a large star nozzle and pipe 12–14 small shapes onto greased baking sheets. Bake in the oven for 10–15 minutes until the biscuits are light brown. Transfer to wire racks to cool. Use the jam to sandwich together pairs of the biscuits and dust with icing sugar.

CHERRY OAT BISCUITS

3 oz (75 g) plain flour
½ tsp bicarbonate of soda
2 oz (50 g) glacé cherries, chopped
3 oz (75 g) caster sugar
3 oz (75 g) rolled oats
4 oz (110 g) butter
1 tbsp golden syrup
1 tbsp milk

Preheat the oven to 300°F/150°C/Gas Mk 2. Sift the flour and bicarbonate of soda together in a bowl. Add the cherries, sugar and rolled oats and mix thoroughly. Place the butter and syrup in a small saucepan and heat gently until the butter has melted. Pour in the milk, stirring well, then remove from the heat and mix into the flour mixture. Mix well until thoroughly blended. Chill in the refrigerator for 5 minutes. Make small balls of the dough and arrange on lightly greased baking sheets, leaving room for the biscuits to spread. Press down the top of each ball and bake in the oven for 20–25 minutes until golden brown. Leave to cool on the baking sheets for a few minutes, then transfer to wire racks to cool completely.

MOCHA COOKIES

8 oz (225 g) butter
4 oz (110 g) caster sugar
8 oz (225 g) self-raising flour
2 oz (50 g) cocoa powder

Filling:
2 oz (50 g) cocoa powder
¼ pint (150 ml) strong coffee
2 oz (50 g) butter
sugar to taste

Preheat the oven to 350°F/180°C/Gas Mk 4. Cream the butter and sugar together in a bowl. Add the flour and cocoa powder, and mix thoroughly until stiff. Using lightly floured hands, form the mixture into walnut-sized balls and arrange on lightly greased baking trays. Gently press down the top of each ball. Bake in the oven for 12 minutes. Carefully transfer to wire racks to cool. To make the filling, place the coffee and cocoa powder in a saucepan and heat until the mixture is a thick cream. Remove from the heat and beat in the butter, adding sugar to taste. Set aside to cool and then use this mixture to sandwich the biscuits together.

COCONUT AND LEMON PYRAMIDS
Makes 10

2 egg whites
5 oz (150 g) caster sugar
6 oz (175 g) desiccated coconut
finely grated zest of 1 lemon

Preheat the oven to 350°F/180°C/Gas Mk 4. Whisk the egg whites until they form stiff peaks, then add half the caster sugar and beat again. Fold in the remaining caster sugar, together with the coconut and lemon zest. Take two tablespoonfuls of the mixture, shape into a pyramid and place on a baking sheet lined with greaseproof paper. Continue in this way until all the mixture is used up. Bake above the centre of a preheated oven for 15–20 minutes until the tops are just golden brown. Lift the lining paper with the coconut pyramids onto a wire cooling tray. Leave to cool before removing from the paper.

MACAROONS
Makes 16

2 large egg whites
4 oz (110 g) ground almonds
6 oz (175 g) caster sugar
1 oz (25 g) ground rice
few drops almond essence
8 blanched almonds

Preheat the oven to 300°F/150°C/Gas Mk 2. Line two large baking sheets with rice paper. Place 1 tsp of the egg white in a bowl and set aside. Place the remaining egg white in a bowl and whisk until it forms soft peaks. Fold in the almonds, sugar and ground rice, and add almond essence to taste. Mix thoroughly. Arrange about sixteen heaped teaspoons of the mixture on the rice paper, pressing down the tops slightly. Place half a blanched almond on top of each one and brush them with the reserved egg white. Bake in the oven for 25–30 minutes until golden brown. Leave to cool slightly on the baking trays before cutting away the excess rice paper from around each macaroon. When the macaroons are completely cold, store them in an airtight tin.

TEA BREADS

TREACLE LOAF
Makes a 2 lb (1 kg) loaf

8 oz (225 g) plain wholemeal flour
8 oz (225 g) plain white flour
4 oz (110 g) sugar
5 oz (150 g) seedless raisins
1 oz (25 g) chopped mixed nuts
6 oz (175 g) black treacle
½ pt (300 ml) milk
½ tsp bicarbonate of soda
1 egg, beaten

Preheat the oven to 350°F/180°C/Gas Mk 4. Grease a 2 lb (1 kg) loaf tin and line with greased greaseproof paper. Sift the flours into a bowl, add the sugar, raisins and nuts and mix well. Heat the treacle and milk together in a saucepan until lukewarm. Add the bicarbonate of soda to the liquid, then add the liquid to the dry ingredients. Add the egg and beat well. Pour into the tin and bake for 1½ hours. Cool on a wire rack.

CIDER BREAD
Makes a 2 lb (1 kg) loaf

12 oz (350 g) mixed dried fruit
½ pt (300 ml) sweet cider
10 oz (300 g) self-raising flour, sifted
6 oz (175 g) light soft brown sugar
2 oz (50 g) shelled walnuts, chopped
2 eggs, beaten

Place the dried fruit in a bowl and pour over the cider. Cover and leave to stand for 12 hours. Transfer to a saucepan and bring to the boil. Remove from the heat and leave to cool. Grease a 2 lb (1 kg) loaf tin, line the base with greaseproof paper and preheat the oven to 350°F/180°C/Gas Mk 4. Sift the flour into a bowl and stir in the sugar and walnuts. Beat in the cider and fruit mixture and the eggs. Put the mixture into the tin and bake for 30 minutes. Reduce oven temperature to 325°F/170°C/Gas Mk 3 and continue baking for 45 minutes. Cool on a wire rack.

PINEAPPLE BREAD
Makes a 2 lb (1 kg) loaf

4 oz (110 g) butter
2 oz (50 g) caster sugar
3 tbsp black treacle
1 egg, beaten
12 oz (350 g) self-raising flour, sifted
8 oz (225 g) can pineapple in natural juice
2 oz (50 g) shelled walnuts, chopped
6 oz (175 g) icing sugar, sifted

Preheat the oven to 350°F/180°C/Gas Mk 4. Grease a 2 lb (1 kg) loaf tin and line with greased greaseproof paper. Drain the pineapple, reserving the juice, and chop the pineapple chunks coarsely. Cream together the butter, sugar and treacle until light and fluffy. Gradually beat the egg into the mixture with a little of the flour to prevent curdling. Fold in the remaining flour, together with the chopped pineapple, walnuts and 4 tbsp of the pineapple juice. Turn into the loaf tin, place in a greaseproof paper bag and bake in the oven for 1 hour. Leave in the tin for 10 minutes, then remove and cool on a wire rack. Mix the icing sugar with 2 tbsp of the pineapple juice and spread over the top of the loaf when it is cold.

MALTED FRUIT BREAD
Makes a 2 lb (1 kg) loaf

1 lb (450 g) self-raising flour, sifted
2 tsp bicarbonate of soda
pinch of salt
½ pt (300 ml) milk
4 tbsp malt extract
4 tbsp golden syrup
8 oz (225 g) sultanas
2 eggs, beaten

Preheat the oven to 350°F/180°C/Gas Mk 4. Grease a 2 lb (1 kg) loaf tin and line the base with greased greaseproof paper. Sift the flour, bicarbonate of soda and salt into a bowl. In a saucepan, heat the milk with the malt and syrup until lukewarm. Add to the flour and mix well, then stir in the sultanas. Turn into the tin and bake for 1¼ hours. Cool on a wire rack.

APPLE AND NUT BREAD
Makes a 2 lb (1 kg) loaf

8 oz (225 g) self-raising flour, sifted
1 tsp baking powder
½ tsp ground cinnamon
pinch of ground nutmeg
2 oz (50 g) shelled walnuts, finely chopped
3 oz (75 g) butter
5 oz (150 g) light soft brown sugar
2 eggs
2 tbsp milk
1½ oz (40 g) seedless raisins
1 cooking apple, peeled, cored and diced
4 oz (110 g) icing sugar
a little warm water

Preheat the oven to 350°F/180°C/Gas Mk 4. Grease a 2 lb (1 kg) loaf tin and line with greased greaseproof paper. Sift the flour, baking powder and spices into a bowl and stir in the chopped walnuts. Cream the butter and sugar until fluffy. Beat the eggs and milk together. Add the dry ingredients to the butter mixture, then add the egg mixture. Stir the raisins and the apple into the mixture. Turn into the tin and bake for 1 hour. Cool on a wire rack. Mix the icing sugar with a little warm water and spread over the top of the loaf when it is cold.

NUTTY BREAD
Makes a 1 lb (450 g) loaf

6 oz (175 g) self-raising flour, sifted
pinch of salt
2 oz (50 g) porridge oats
4 oz (110 g) soft light brown sugar
4 oz (110 g) butter
3 oz (75 g) shelled walnuts, chopped
2 eggs, beaten
4 tbsp milk

Preheat the oven to 350°F/180°C/Gas Mk 4. Grease a 1 lb (450 g) loaf tin and line the base with greased greaseproof paper. Sift the flour and salt into a bowl, and stir in the oats and sugar. Rub in the butter until the mixture resembles fine breadcrumbs, then stir in the walnuts. Add the beaten eggs and milk, mix well and bake in the oven for 1¼ hours. Cool on a wire rack.

HONEY FRUIT BREAD
Makes a 1 lb (450 g) loaf

6 oz (175 g) plain flour, sifted
3 oz (75 g) demerara sugar
1 tsp bicarbonate of soda
1 tsp mixed spice
pinch of salt
1 oz (25 g) margarine
1 egg, beaten
3 oz (75 g) clear honey
¼ pt (150 ml) water
2 oz (50 g) currants or sultanas

Preheat the oven to 350°F/180°C/Gas Mk 4. Grease a 1 lb (450 g) loaf tin and line the base with greased greaseproof paper. Sift the flour into a bowl and stir in the sugar, bicarbonate of soda, spice and salt, then rub in the margarine. Mix the egg, honey and water in a bowl, then beat this into the flour mixture, followed by the currants or sultanas. Turn into the tin and bake about 1¼ hours. Cool on a wire rack.

COTTAGE CHEESE AND FRUIT TEA BREAD
Makes a 1 lb (450 g) loaf

8 oz (225 g) self-raising flour, sifted
pinch of salt
½ tsp mixed spice
1 oz (25 g) sugar
2 oz (50 g) butter
2 eggs
4 oz (110 g) cottage cheese
4 tbsp milk
1 oz (25 g) walnuts, chopped
2 oz (50 g) sultanas

Preheat the oven to 350°F/180°C/Gas Mk 4. Sift the flour, salt and mixed spice into a bowl. Stir in the sugar and rub in the butter until the mixture resembles fine breadcrumbs. Beat the eggs with the cheese and milk, then add to the flour mixture, together with the walnuts and sultanas. Mix thoroughly and turn into a greased 1 lb (450 g) loaf tin. Cook in the oven for 45 minutes or until well risen and golden brown. Leave to cool in the tin for 5 minutes and then turn out onto a wire rack to cool completely.

DATE BREAD
Makes a 2 lb (1 kg) loaf

8 oz (225 g) stoned dates, chopped
6 fl oz (175 ml) cold tea
8 oz (225 g) plain wholemeal flour
6 oz (175 g) soft light brown sugar
4 tsp baking powder
1 tsp mixed spice
1 egg, beaten
1 oz (25 g) demerara sugar

Grease a 2 lb (1 kg) loaf tin and line the base with greased grease-proof paper. In a bowl mix together the tea and chopped dates, and leave to stand for 2 hours. Preheat the oven to 350°F/180°C/Gas Mk 4. Sift the flour, baking powder and spice into a separate bowl. Add the sugar, then the dates with the tea. Mix well then add the egg. Mix well again, then turn into the tin. Sprinkle the demerara sugar on top and bake in the oven for 1¼ hours. Remove from the oven, cool in the tin for 5 minutes then turn out onto a wire rack.

GINGERED PEANUT LOAF
Makes a 2 lb (1 kg) loaf

12 oz (350 g) self-raising flour, sifted
pinch of salt
1 tsp ground ginger
2 oz (50 g) soft brown sugar
3 oz (75 g) sultanas
2 oz (50 g) preserved stem ginger, chopped
3 oz (75 g) unsalted peanuts
3 oz (75 g) unsalted butter
4 tbsp black treacle
2 eggs
¼ pt (150 ml) milk

Preheat the oven to 325°F/170°C/Gas Mk 3. Grease a 2 lb (1 kg) loaf tin and line the base with greased greaseproof paper. Sift the flour, salt and ground ginger into a bowl. Add the sugar, sultanas, stem ginger and peanuts and mix well. Heat the butter and treacle in a small saucepan over a low heat until melted. Add to the flour mixture and then gradually beat in the eggs and milk until all the ingredients are well blended. Pour into the tin and bake for 1¼ hours. Cool slightly then turn out onto a wire rack to cool completely.

CHOPPED PEANUT LOAF
Makes a 2 lb (1 kg) loaf

4 oz (110 g) wholemeal flour
4 oz (110 g) plain flour
2 tbsp baking powder
¼ tsp salt
4 oz (110 g) peanut butter
1 egg
3 tbsp clear honey
8 fl oz (225 ml) milk
1 oz (25 g) margarine, melted
1 tsp grated lemon rind
2 oz (50 g) salted peanuts, chopped

Preheat the oven to 350°F/180°C/Gas Mk 4. Sift together the flours, baking powder and salt in a large bowl. Rub in the peanut butter until the mixture is crumbly. Lightly beat the egg and add to the mixture together with the honey, milk, melted margarine and lemon rind. Stir until all the ingredients are combined, then fold in the chopped peanuts. Turn the mixture into a greased 2 lb (1 kg) loaf tin and bake in the oven for 1 hour. Cool for 10 minutes in the tin, then turn out onto a wire rack to cool completely.

BANANA BREAD
Makes a 2 lb (1 kg) loaf

8 oz (225 g) self-raising flour
½ tsp salt
3 oz (75 g) margarine
5 oz (150 g) light soft brown sugar
2 eggs
1 tbsp golden syrup, warmed
3 medium bananas, mashed
2 oz (50 g) seedless raisins
1½ oz (40 g) chopped mixed nuts

Preheat oven to 350°F/180°C/Gas Mk 4. Sift the flour and salt into a bowl, then rub in the margarine until the mixture resembles fine breadcrumbs. Stir in the sugar, beat in the eggs and add the warm syrup to the mixture. Work the mashed bananas into the flour mixture, then add the raisins and nuts. Turn the mixture into a well greased 2 lb (1 kg) loaf tin and bake in the oven for 1½ hours. Cool on a wire rack. If possible, store in an airtight container or wrap in foil for a day or two before eating, as this improves the flavour.

ORANGE AND WALNUT LOAF
Makes a 1lb (450 g) loaf

6 oz (175 g) self-raising flour, sifted
1 tsp baking powder
grated rind and juice of 1 large orange
2 oz (50 g) walnuts, chopped
2 oz (50 g) candied peel, chopped
3 oz (75 g) soft margarine
3 oz (75 g) soft light brown sugar
1 egg, beaten
3 tbsp milk

Preheat the oven to 350°F/180°C/Gas Mk 4. Grease a 1 lb (450 g) loaf tin and line the base with greaseproof paper. Place all the ingredients in a large mixing bowl and beat until thoroughly blended. Turn the mixture into the tin and bake for 1 hour until well risen. Leave to cool in the tin for 15 minutes, then turn out onto a wire rack.

COUNTRY NUT LOAF
Makes a 2 lb (1 kg) loaf

6 oz (175 g) butter or soft margarine
6 oz (175 g) caster sugar
3 large eggs, beaten
8 oz (225 g) self-raising flour, sifted
1 oz (25 g) ground almonds
3 oz (75 g) mixed chopped nuts
2 tbsp milk
2 tbsp apricot jam

Preheat the oven to 325°F/170°C/Gas Mk 3. Grease a 2 lb (1 kg) loaf tin and line the base with greaseproof paper. Cream the butter or margarine together with the caster sugar until light and fluffy. Beat in the eggs one at a time, using a little flour to bind if the mixture starts to curdle. Fold the flour into the creamed mixture alternately with the ground almonds. Gently stir in the mixed nuts, adding just enough milk to make a soft, but fairly stiff dough, and spoon the mixture into the tin, levelling the top. Bake in the centre of the oven for 1¼-1½ hours, or until a warm skewer inserted into the cake comes out clean. Turn out and leave to cool on a wire rack. When cold, brush with 2 tablespoons of warmed, sieved apricot jam. Leave to set before cutting.

CHOCOLATE TOPPED ORANGE LOAF
Makes a 2 lb (1 kg) loaf

6 oz (175 g) soft margarine
6 oz (175 g) caster sugar
6 oz (175 g) self-raising flour
1 tsp baking powder
grated rind of 1 orange
3 eggs, beaten
2 tbsp milk

Chocolate topping:
2 oz (50 g) hard margarine
2 tbsp cocoa powder, sifted
1 tbsp golden syrup

Preheat the oven to 375°F/190°C/Gas Mk 5. Grease a 2 lb (1 kg) loaf tin lined with greased greaseproof paper. Place the margarine, caster sugar, flour, baking powder, orange rind, eggs and milk in a bowl and mix well until all the ingredients are thoroughly blended. Turn the mixture into the tin and bake for 1 hour until well risen. Leave to cool in the tin before turning out and removing the paper. In a small saucepan, melt the hard margarine, cocoa powder and syrup, stirring all the time. Remove from the heat and leave to cool. When the mixture is just beginning to set, spread evenly over the top of the loaf.

WELSH CURRANT LOAF
Makes a 2 lb (1 kg) loaf

6 oz (175 g) currants
6 oz (175 g) sultanas
½ pt (300 ml) cider
5 oz (150 g) self-raising flour
5 oz (150 g) wholemeal flour
2 tsp baking powder
8 oz (225 g) soft light brown sugar
1 egg, beaten

Put the currants and sultanas in a bowl, pour over the cider, cover with clingfilm and leave overnight. Grease a 2 lb (1 kg) loaf tin and line with greased greaseproof paper. Preheat the oven to 300°F/150°C/Gas Mk 2. Add the sifted flours, baking powder, sugar and egg to the fruit and cider mixture and beat well. Turn the mixture into the tin and level the top. Bake for 1¾ hours until well risen. Leave in the tin for a few minutes then turn out onto wire rack to cool.

DATE AND WALNUT LOAF 1
Makes a 2 lb (1 kg) loaf

4 oz (110 g) self-raising flour
4 oz (110 g) wholemeal flour
2 tsp baking powder
4 oz (110 g) soft margarine
4 oz (110 g) soft light brown sugar
1 tsp mixed spice
8 oz (225 g) fresh dates, stoned and chopped
5 tbsp milk
1 egg, beaten

Preheat the oven to 325°F/170°C/Gas Mk 3. Grease a 2 lb (1 kg) loaf tin and line with greased greaseproof paper. Put all the ingredients in a large mixing bowl and beat well. Turn the mixture into the tin and level the top. Bake for 1½ hours until well risen. Leave to cool completely in the tin before turning out.

DATE AND WALNUT LOAF 2
Makes a 2 lb (1 kg) loaf

8 oz (225 g) treacle or molasses
12 oz (350 g) wholemeal flour, sifted
6 oz (175 g) plain flour, sifted
8 oz (225 g) soft light brown sugar
2 oz (50 g) walnuts, chopped
8 oz (225 g) chopped dates
1 tsp bicarbonate of soda
1 large cup milk

Preheat the oven to 350°F/180°C/Gas Mk 4. Warm the treacle and then mix together all the ingredients in a large bowl, adding sufficient milk to make the mixture easy to stir, but not too soft. Turn into a greased 2 lb (1 kg) loaf tin, and bake for 1–1½ hours. This loaf is particularly good if left to mature in a tin for 3–4 days before using.

BANANA AND DATE BREAD
Makes a 2 lb (1 kg) loaf

8 oz (225 g) wholemeal flour
2 tsp baking powder
4 oz (110 g) soft margarine
3 oz (75 g) soft light brown sugar
2 eggs, beaten
1 lb (450 g) ripe bananas, peeled and mashed
4 oz (110 g) dates, stoned and chopped

Preheat the oven to 350°F/180°C/Gas Mk 4. Grease and line a 2 lb (1 kg) loaf tin with greased greaseproof paper. Mix the flour, baking powder, margarine, sugar and eggs in a large bowl. Add the mashed bananas. Beat thoroughly until well blended. Add the dates and stir well. Turn the mixture into the tin and bake for 1¼–1½ hours until firm. Leave in the tin for about 5 minutes before turning out onto a wire rack to cool.

PINEAPPLE AND RAISIN BREAD

6 oz (175 g) self raising wholemeal flour
6 oz (175 g) self-raising white flour
pinch of salt
1 tsp cinnamon
2 oz (50 g) soft brown sugar
2 oz (50 g) butter
2 eggs, beaten
¼ pt (150 ml) milk
8 oz (225 g) can pineapple rings, drained
2 oz (50 g) raisins

Preheat the oven to 325°F/170°C/Gas Mk 3. Sift the flours, salt and cinnamon into a large bowl, add the sugar and mix well. Cut in the butter and rub in until thoroughly blended. Gradually beat in the milk and eggs using a wooden spoon. Chop the pineapple slices and stir into the mixture. Stir in the raisins. Turn into a greased 2 lb (1 kg) loaf tin and bake in the oven for 1 hour until golden and firm. Leave in the tin for about 10 minutes before turning out onto a wire rack to cool.

EASY TEA BREAD
Makes a 1 lb (450 g) loaf

8 oz (225 g) mixed dried fruit
¼ pt (150 ml) strong tea
8 oz (225 g) flour, sifted
4 oz (110 g) sugar
1 egg, beaten
milk as needed

Soak the mixed fruit in the tea overnight. Preheat the oven to 375°F/190°C/Gas Mk 5. Beat in the flour, sugar and beaten egg and blend well. Turn into a lightly greased 1 lb (450 g) tin and bake in the oven for 50 minutes. Cool on a wire rack before cutting.

BARA BRITH
Makes a 2 lb (1 kg) loaf

1 oz (25 g) fresh yeast or
½ oz (15 g) dried yeast
1 tsp sugar
½ pt (300 ml) warm milk
1 lb (450 g) wholemeal flour
1 tsp salt
1 tsp mixed spice

3 oz (75 g) butter
2 oz (50 g) brown sugar
3 oz (75 g) raisins
3 oz (75 g) currants
1 oz (25 g) candied peel
honey for glazing

Grease a 2 lb (1 kg) loaf tin and line the base with greased greaseproof paper. Crumble the yeast onto the tepid milk. If using dried yeast, dissolve the 1 tsp sugar in a little warm milk and sprinkle in the yeast. Leave for about 15 minutes in a warm place until frothy. Sift the flour, salt and mixed spice into a large bowl and rub in the butter until the mixture resembles fine breadcrumbs. Make a well in the centre and add the brown sugar and the yeast mixture. Stir well, bringing in the flour from the sides a little at a time. Turn onto a floured board and knead until smooth. Place in a large oiled plastic bag and leave in a warm place until doubled in size (about 1½ hours). Return dough to the floured board and knead again, this time working in the dried fruit and candied peel. Place in the loaf tin and return to the plastic bag. Leave to rise for another 1½ hours or until doubled in size. Preheat the oven to 200°C/400°F/Gas Mk 6. Bake for 50–60 minutes. Turn out and glaze with a little clear honey. Serve sliced, with butter.

SPICED BREAD
Makes a 1 lb (450 g) loaf

4 oz (110 g) butter or margarine
12 oz (350 g) self-raising flour, sifted
4 oz (110 g) soft brown sugar
2 eggs, beaten
1 tbsp mixed spices
2 oz (50 g) sultanas
2 oz (50 g) currants
2 tbsp milk

Preheat the oven to 350°F/180°C/Gas Mk 4. Rub the fat into the flour until the mixture resembles fine breadcrumbs, and then stir in the remaining dry ingredients. Mix in the eggs, adding a little milk to make a stiff batter. Pour into a well greased 1 lb (450 g) loaf tin and bake for about 1 hour or until the centre of the bread is cooked.

MUESLI LOAF
Makes a 2 lb (1 kg) loaf

1 oz (25 g) fresh yeast or 1 tbsp dried yeast
1 tsp clear honey
8 fl oz (250 ml) warm milk
1 lb (450 g) plain wholemeal flour
1 tsp salt
2 oz (50 g) butter
1 egg, beaten
6 oz (175 g) muesli

Grease a 2 lb (1 kg) loaf tin. Stir the yeast and honey into the warm milk. If using dried yeast leave to stand in the milk for 5 minutes. Stir in 4 oz (110 g) of the flour and leave in a warm place for about 30 minutes or until the mixture becomes frothy. Sift together the remaining flour and salt and rub in the butter until the mixture resembles fine breadcrumbs. Stir the flour mixture and the egg into the yeast mixture and mix to a soft dough. Turn onto a floured board and knead until smooth. Place in a lightly oiled plastic bag and leave in a warm place for about 1 hour, or until doubled in size. Turn out onto the floured board again and work in the muesli until evenly distributed. Roll to fit the loaf tin and place in the tin inside the plastic bag. Leave in a warm place again for another hour, or until risen and springy to touch. Preheat the oven to 400°F/200°C/Gas Mk 6. Bake for about 50 minutes until the loaf is golden brown and sounds hollow when tapped on the base. Cool on a wire rack.

SYRUP AND NUT BREAD
Makes a 1 lb (450 g) loaf

¼ pt (150 ml) milk
2 heaped tbsp golden syrup or honey
8 oz (225 g) self-raising flour, sifted
1 level tsp bicarbonate of soda
pinch of salt
3 oz (75 g) chopped dates
1½ oz (40 g) chopped nuts

Preheat the oven to 350°F/180°C/Gas Mk 4. Warm the milk and syrup or honey together over a gentle heat. Sift the flour and bicarbonate of soda together with a pinch of salt and stir into the warmed milk mixture. Stir in the chopped dates and nuts, reserving a handful of nuts. The consistency should be like a stiff batter. Pour into the tin and sprinkle the reserved nuts on top. Bake for about 1 hour until a skewer inserted into the centre of the loaf comes out clean.

IRISH TREACLE LOAF
Makes a 1 lb (450 g) loaf

2 oz (50 g) butter
4 tbsp water
1 heaped tbsp black treacle
2 oz (50 g) soft brown sugar
1 egg, beaten
8 oz (225 g) flour, sifted
½ tsp mixed spice
½ tsp ground ginger
1 level tsp bicarbonate of soda
pinch of salt
2 oz (50 g) raisins
2 oz (50 g) currants

Preheat the oven to 350°F/180°C/Gas Mk 4. Heat the water with the butter in a pan over a low heat. When the butter has melted remove from the heat and gradually add the treacle, sugar and egg and beat together. Sift the flour, mixed spice, ginger, bicarbonate of soda and a pinch of salt into a bowl. Stir in the treacle mixture, add the fruit and mix well. Turn into a greased 1 lb (450 g) loaf tin and bake for about 1½ hours until firm to the touch.

APRICOT AND WALNUT LOAF
Makes a 1 lb (450 g) loaf

4 oz (110 g) wholemeal flour, sifted
4 oz (110 g) strong white flour, sifted
1 tsp salt
knob of lard
1 oz (25 g) caster sugar
4 oz (110 g) dried apricots, chopped
2 oz (50 g) walnuts, roughly chopped
¼ oz (5 g) fresh yeast
¼ pt (150 ml) water

Topping:
1 oz (25 g) butter
1 oz (25 g) caster sugar
1½ oz (40 g) plain flour

Grease a 1 lb (450 g) loaf tin and line the base with greaseproof paper. Sift the flours and salt into a large bowl. Rub in the lard, then stir in the sugar, apricots and walnuts. Blend the yeast with the water and add to the mixture. Mix to a soft, scone-like mixture, leaving the sides of the bowl clean. Add more flour if the mixture appears too moist. Turn into the prepared tin and put it inside a plastic bag in a warm place until the dough rises to within ½ inch (10 mm) of the top of the tin. To make the topping, lightly rub together the butter, sugar and flour until the mixture resembles coarse breadcrumbs and cover the top of the loaf with this mixture. Preheat the oven to 400°F/200°C/Gas Mk 6. Bake in the centre of the oven for 40-45 minutes. Cool in the tin for 10 minutes, then turn out onto a wire rack.

CHERRY AND BANANA BREAD
Makes a 2 lb (1 kg) loaf

8 oz (225 g) self-raising flour, sifted
pinch of salt
4 oz (110 g) soft margarine
6 oz (175 g) soft brown sugar

2 large eggs, beaten
2 ripe bananas
4 oz (110 g) glacé cherries,
washed and chopped

Preheat the oven to 350°F/180°C/Gas Mk 4. Grease a 2 lb (1 kg) loaf tin and line the base with greaseproof paper. Sift the flour and salt into a bowl and add the margarine, sugar, beaten eggs, mashed bananas and cherries. Mix well to combine all the ingredients and then beat for a minute. Turn into the tin and level the top. Bake in the centre of the oven for about 1¼–1½ hours. Cool completely before cutting.

DUTCH HONEY AND SPICE LOAF
Makes a 2 lb (1 kg) loaf

5 oz (150 g) soured cream
4 oz (110 g) soft brown sugar
1 large egg
9 oz (250 g) wholemeal flour
1 level tsp bicarbonate of soda
2 level tsp ground cinnamon
4 level tbsp clear honey
3 oz (75 g) margarine
1 oz (25 g) flaked almonds

Grease a 2 lb (1 kg) loaf tin and line the base with greaseproof paper. Preheat the oven to 300°F/150°C/Gas Mk 2. Put the soured cream into a bowl and beat in the sugar and egg. Sift the flour, bicarbonate of soda and cinnamon together and fold into the soured cream mixture. Gently heat the honey and margarine until it melts, then stir into the mixture. Transfer to the prepared tin, level the top and sprinkle over the flaked almonds. Bake in the centre of the oven for about 1½ hours until springy to the touch. Cool in the tin. Serve sliced and buttered.

MALT LOAF
Makes 2 x 1 lb (450 g) loaves

2 oz (50 g) margarine
3 oz (75 g) granulated sugar
3 tbsp golden syrup
3 tbsp malt extract
¼ pt (150 ml) milk
10 oz (300 g) self-raising flour, sifted
¼ level tsp bicarbonate of soda
4 oz (110 g) mixed dried fruit

Grease and line two 1 lb (450 g) loaf tins. Preheat the oven to 350°F/180°C/Gas Mk 4. Gently melt the margarine, sugar, golden syrup, malt extract and milk in a saucepan and stir. Sift the flour and bicarbonate of soda into a bowl, then stir in the dried fruit. Pour the melted mixture onto the dry ingredients and mix. Divide the mixture between the two tins. Bake just above the centre of the oven for 50 minutes or until firm to the touch and a skewer inserted into the centre comes out clean. Cool in the tin for 20 minutes, then turn out onto a wire tray. Store in an airtight tin or wrap in greaseproof paper and cover with foil.

WALNUT LOAF
Makes a 2 lb (1 kg) loaf

10 oz (300 g) plain flour, sifted
1 tsp salt
2 tsp cream of tartar
2 oz (50 g) chopped walnuts
1 egg
5 oz (150 g) soft light brown sugar
1 tsp bicarbonate of soda
½ pt (300 ml) milk

Grease a 2 lb (1 kg) loaf tin. Sift together the flour, salt and cream of tartar and add the walnuts. Break the egg into another bowl and add the sugar, bicarbonate of soda and milk. Beat thoroughly with an egg whisk. Gradually add the flour mixture to the egg mixture and stir well. (The mixture will be quite wet.) Pour into the tin and leave for about 15 minutes. Meanwhile preheat the oven to 350°F/180°C/ Gas Mk 4. Bake for about 1 hour. When a skewer inserted into the centre of the loaf comes out clean, the loaf is ready. If the skewer is still moist, cook a little longer. Cool on a wire rack.

CINNAMON LOAF
Makes a 1 lb (450 g) loaf

8 oz (225 g) self-raising flour, sifted
1 level tsp ground cinnamon
2 oz (50 g) butter, cut into small pieces
2 oz (50 g) caster sugar
1 large egg, beaten
2 level tbsp golden syrup
2 level tbsp milk

Preheat the oven to 350°F/180°C/Gas Mk 4. Grease and line the base of a 1 lb (450 g) loaf tin. Sift the flour and cinnamon into a bowl and add the butter. Rub in the butter until the mixture resembles fine breadcrumbs, then stir in the caster sugar. Add the egg and syrup to the mixture, and enough milk to give a fairly soft consistency. Turn into the tin and level the top. Bake in the centre of the oven for about 45 minutes. Cool completely before cutting.

JAMAICAN TEA LOAF
Makes a 2 lb (1 kg) loaf

2 oz (50 g) soft margarine
3 oz (75 g) caster sugar
6 level tbsp black treacle
3 oz (75 g) plain flour, sifted
2 level tsp baking powder
pinch of salt
8 oz (225 g) wholemeal flour, sifted
1 tsp ground ginger
3 oz (75 g) sultanas
8 fl oz (225 ml) milk
icing sugar for dredging

Preheat the oven to 350°F/180°C/Gas Mk 4. Grease and base line a 2 lb (1 kg) loaf tin. Cream together the margarine and sugar until light and fluffy and then beat in the treacle. Sift together the plain flour, baking powder and salt, mix them into the wholemeal flour and add the ground ginger. Fold the sultanas into the creamed mixture and then add the flour and the milk alternately, stirring well between each addition. Place in the prepared tin and level the top. Bake for about 1¼ hours on the centre shelf of the oven. Cool on a wire tray and dust with icing sugar.

APRICOT AND PRUNE LOAF
Makes a 2 lb (1 kg) loaf

2 oz (50 g) dried apricots, chopped
2 oz (50 g) dried prunes, stoned and chopped
grated rind of 1 orange
6 oz (175 g) self-raising flour, sifted
4 oz (110 g) butter
4 oz (110 g) caster sugar
2 large eggs

Preheat the oven to 325°F/170°C/Gas Mk 3. Grease a 2 lb (1 kg) loaf tin and line the base. Mix the fruit together with the orange rind and mix in 1 tbsp of the flour. Cream the butter and sugar together until soft and fluffy. Add the eggs, one at a time, beating well after each addition. Fold the flour into the creamed mixture with a metal spoon. Stir in 2 tbsp warm water and the fruit. Turn the mixture into the tin, and make a hollow in the centre. Bake in the centre of the oven for 1¼ hours or until a skewer inserted in the centre of the loaf comes out clean. Turn out onto a wire tray, remove the paper and leave to cool.

BRACK BREAD
Makes a 2 lb (1 kg) loaf

8 oz (225 g) raisins
8 oz (225 g) sultanas
¼ pint (150 ml) hot tea
8 oz (225 g) soft dark brown sugar
8 oz (225 g) self-raising wheatmeal flour
2 tsp ground mixed spice
2 eggs, beaten

Preheat the oven to 350°F/180°C/Gas Mk 4. Put the raisins and sultanas in a bowl, pour over the hot tea and leave for at least 1 hour. Stir in the sugar, flour, mixed spice and beaten eggs and mix well. Grease a 2 lb (1 kg) loaf tin, line the base with greaseproof paper and spoon in the mixture. Level the top and bake in the centre of the oven for 1 hour or until a skewer inserted in the centre of the loaf comes out clean. Turn out and cool on a wire rack. Serve cold, sliced and buttered.

ORANGE TREACLE LOAF
Makes a 2 lb (1 kg) loaf

8 oz (225 g) plain flour
1 level tsp bicarbonate of soda
2 level tsp cinnamon
4 oz (110 g) margarine
4 oz (110 g) dark brown sugar
2 level tbsp golden syrup
2 level tbsp treacle
grated rind and juice of 1 large orange
1 egg, beaten

Preheat the oven to 325°F/170°C/Gas Mk 3. Grease a 2 lb (1 kg) loaf tin and line the base with greaseproof paper. Sift the flour, bicarbonate of soda and cinnamon into a bowl. Put the margarine, sugar, golden syrup and treacle into a large saucepan and heat gently until the fat has melted. Remove from the heat, add the orange rind and juice, followed by the egg and then the flour mixture. Beat well with a wooden spoon until a smooth, batter-like consistency is achieved. Pour the mixture into the tin and bake just below the centre of the oven for 1 hour, or until the cake is firm to the touch. Turn out onto a wire rack and leave to cool.

MARMALADE TEABREAD
Makes 2 x 1 lb (450 g) loaves

4 oz (110 g) margarine or butter
12 oz (350 g) self-raising flour, sifted
3 oz (75 g) caster sugar
1 oz (25 g) mixed peel
¼ pt (150 ml) milk
4 tbsp thin-cut marmalade
1 egg, beaten

Topping:
1 oz (25 g) caster sugar
1 oz (25 g) mixed peel

Grease and base-line two 1 lb (450 g) loaf tins. Preheat the oven to 350°F/180°C/Gas Mk 4. Rub the margarine or butter into the flour until the mixture resembles fine breadcrumbs. Stir in the sugar and the peel. Mix together the milk, marmalade and egg. Beat thoroughly to break up any large lumps of marmalade. Stir into the flour mixture and divide between the two tins. To make the topping, mix together the sugar and mixed peel and sprinkle over the loaf. Bake in the centre of the oven for about 50 minutes, or until a skewer inserted into the centre of the bread comes out clean. Remove from the tin when cold.

COCONUT BREAD
Makes a 2 lb (1 kg) loaf

1 lb (450 g) strong plain white flour, sifted
½ tsp salt
3 oz (75 g) desiccated coconut
1 oz (25 g) sugar
½ oz (15 g) fresh yeast or ¼ oz (5 g) dried yeast
½ pt (300 ml) warm milk
a little clear honey to glaze

Sift the flour and salt into a bowl and stir in the coconut, reserving 2 tsp. Mix in the sugar, reserving 1 tsp. Mix the yeast with the reserved sugar and warm milk and leave until frothy. Mix into the flour to form a dough and knead well. Cover and leave for about 1 hour. Knead the dough again, shape and fit into a greased 2 lb (1 kg) loaf tin. Cover and leave for 30 minutes. Preheat the oven to 400°F/200°C/Gas Mk 6. Bake the loaf for 40 minutes. While the loaf is still hot, brush over the top with a wet brush dipped in honey and sprinkle over the reserved coconut. Cool on a wire rack.

ORANGE BREAD
Make a 2 lb (1 kg) loaf

1 lb (450 g) strong plain white flour, sifted
½ tsp salt
1 oz (25 g) sugar
½ oz (15 g) fresh yeast or ¼ oz (5 g) dried yeast
¼ pt (150 ml) warm water
grated rind and juice of 1 large orange
1 egg, beaten
6 oz (175 g) sultanas
a little clear honey to glaze

Sift the flour and salt into a bowl. Stir in the sugar, reserving 1 tsp. In another bowl, mix the yeast and warm water together with the 1 tsp of sugar and leave until frothy. Add the orange rind, orange juice, egg and sultanas to the flour and mix thoroughly. Add the yeast and water mixture to the flour. Knead well, cover and leave for 1 hour. Knead the mixture again, shape and fit into a 2 lb (1 kg) greased loaf tin. Cover and leave for 30 minutes. Preheat the oven to 400°F/200°C/Gas Mk 6. Bake the loaf for 40 minutes. While the loaf is still hot, brush the top with a wet brush dipped in honey. Cool on a wire rack.

GINGERBREAD
Makes a 2 lb (1 kg) loaf

4 oz (110 g) soft margarine
4 oz (110 g) soft dark brown sugar
4 oz (110 g) black treacle
6 oz (175 g) plain flour
2 level tsp ground ginger

1½ level tsp ground cinnamon
1 large egg, beaten
¼ pt (150 ml) milk
1 level tsp bicarbonate of soda

Preheat the oven to 300°F/150°C/Gas Mk 2. Melt the margarine, brown sugar and treacle in a pan over a low heat. Do not allow to boil. Grease and line the base of a 2 lb (1 kg) loaf tin. Sift the flour, ground ginger and cinnamon into a bowl, then stir in the melted margarine, sugar and treacle, followed by the egg. Warm the milk, pour it onto the bicarbonate of soda, stir well and mix into the other ingredients. Pour the mixture into the tin and bake in the centre of the oven for about 2 hours. Cover the top with a piece of greaseproof paper after the first hour. The gingerbread is cooked when it feels firm to the touch and has shrunk away from the sides of the tin.

BRIOCHES
Makes 12

½ oz (15 g) fresh yeast
2 tbsp water
8 oz (225 g) strong plain flour
½ level tsp salt

½ oz (15 g) caster sugar
2 eggs, beaten
2 oz (50 g) butter, melted
  and cooled

Egg wash: 1 egg, beaten
      1 tbsp water

Preheat the oven to 450°F/230°C/Gas Mk 8. Blend the yeast with
2 tbsp water. Sift the flour and salt into a large bowl and add the
sugar. Add the yeast liquid, eggs and butter, and work to a smooth
dough. Turn onto a lightly floured surface and knead well for about
5 minutes. Put the dough in a greased plastic bag and leave to rise at
room temperature for 1–1½ hours. Grease twelve 3 inch (7.5 cm) bun
tins. Divide the risen dough into four equal pieces and then divide
each of these into three equal pieces. Shape about three-quarters of
each piece into a ball and press the remaining small ball in the centre
of the larger one. Repeat this with the remaining pieces, put the bun
trays back into the plastic bag and leave to rise in a warm place for
about 1 hour until the dough has doubled in size. Mix together the
egg and water for the egg wash. Brush the risen brioches with the egg
wash and bake in the centre of the oven for 10 minutes. Serve warm.

GRANNY LOAF
Makes 2 x 2 lb (1 kg) loaves

1 lb 12 oz (800 g) strong plain white flour, sifted
1 tsp ground cinnamon
1 tsp mace
1 tsp ground ginger
½ tsp ground nutmeg
8 oz (225 g) dark soft brown sugar
4 oz (110 g) butter
4 oz (110 g) lard
1 oz (25 g) fresh yeast or ½ oz (15 g) dried yeast
¾ pint (450 ml) tepid milk and water
1 egg, beaten
12 oz (350 g) currants
6 oz (175 g) stoned raisins
6 oz (175 g) sultanas
2 oz (50 g) chopped mixed peel

Sift the flour and spices into a bowl. Reserve 1 tsp of sugar and then stir in the remainder. Rub in the lard and butter until the mixture resembles fine breadcrumbs. Mix the yeast with the reserved sugar, the milk and water and leave until frothy. Then add the yeast mixture to the flour and spice mixture. Add the egg to the flour and spice mixture and work to a soft dough. Knead well, cover and leave to rise for 1 hour. Mix the dried fruit and peel into the dough and knead well. Divide the dough in half, shape and fit into two greased 2 lb (1 kg) loaf tins. Cover and leave for 45 minutes. Preheat the oven to 425°F/220°C/Gas Mk 7. Bake for 20 minutes, then reduce the oven heat to 375°F/190°C/Gas Mk 5 and continue baking for 1 hour. Cool on a wire rack.

SAVOURY BREADS

CHEESE AND HERB BREAD
Makes a 1 lb (450 g) loaf

8 oz (225 g) self-raising flour, sifted
1 tsp baking powder
1 tsp mustard powder
½ tsp salt
pinch of paprika pepper
1 tbsp chopped fresh herbs
3 oz (75 g) soft margarine
1 egg
¼ pint (150 ml) milk
3 oz (75 g) Cheddar cheese, grated

Preheat the oven to 375°F/190°C/Gas Mk 5. Sift the flour, baking powder, mustard powder, salt and paprika pepper into a large bowl, then stir in the herbs. Add the margarine, egg, milk and cheese and mix all the ingredients for 2–3 minutes Spoon the mixture into a greased 1 lb (450 g) loaf tin, smooth the top, and bake in the oven for 45 minutes. Turn out onto a wire rack to cool. Serve hot or cold.

POTATO BREAD
Makes 2 x 1 lb (450 g) loaves

8 oz (225 g) raw potatoes, peeled and grated
8 oz (225 g) cooked potato, cooled and mashed
8 oz (225 g) plain white flour, sifted
½ tsp salt
pinch of pepper
2 oz (50 g) butter, melted

Preheat the oven to 300°F/150°C/Gas Mk 2. Mix the raw and mashed potatoes together then stir in the flour, salt, pepper and melted fat. Mix well but do not knead. Divide the dough into two pieces, press out each piece into a flat round and place on two greased baking sheets. Bake in the oven for 40 minutes. Cut into pieces and serve hot with butter.

CORNBREAD 1
Makes 12 squares

4 oz (110 g) plain flour, sifted
4 oz (110 g) cornmeal
2 tsp baking powder
1 tsp sugar
½ tsp salt
1 egg
8 fl oz (225 ml) milk
3 tbsp melted butter

Preheat the oven to 400°F/200°C/Gas Mk 6. Mix the flour, cornmeal, baking powder, sugar and salt together in a bowl. Beat the egg and milk together in another bowl, then add this mixture to the flour. Stir in the melted butter. Turn the mixture into a greased Swiss roll tin. Bake in the oven for 35 minutes and serve hot.

CORNBREAD 2
Makes 16 slices

4 oz (110 g) wholewheat flour
4 oz (110 g) cornmeal
½ tsp salt
1 tsp bicarbonate of soda
¼ tsp cream of tartar
12 fl oz (350 ml) buttermilk
3 tbsp sunflower oil
2 beaten eggs
1 tbsp brown sugar

Preheat the oven to 425°F/220°C/Gas Mk 7. Sift the flour, cornmeal, salt, bicarbonate of soda and cream of tartar into a large bowl. In another bowl, mix together the buttermilk, oil, eggs and sugar, then pour this into the flour mixture. Stir well. Turn into a greased 8 inch (20 cm) cake tin and bake in the oven for 35 minutes. Cut into 2 inch (5 cm) squares and serve warm.

SODA BREAD
Makes a 2 lb (1 kg) loaf

1 lb (450 g) plain white flour, sifted
1 tsp salt
½ tsp bicarbonate of soda
½ tsp cream of tartar
1 oz (25 g) butter
½ pint (300 ml) buttermilk or sweetened milk

Preheat the oven to 425°F/220°C/Gas Mk 7. Sift the flour, salt, bicarbonate of soda and cream of tartar into a bowl. Rub in the butter and add the milk to form a soft dough. Knead lightly on a floured board. Shape into a round about 2 inches (5 cm) thick. Place on a floured baking sheet and cut a deep cross in the top of the dough. Sprinkle with a little flour and bake in the oven for 25 minutes. Cool on a wire rack.

BAKING POWDER BREAD
Makes 2 x 1 lb (450 g) loaves

1 lb (450 g) plain flour, sifted
1 tbsp baking powder
pinch of salt
½ pt (300 ml) milk and water mixed

Preheat the oven to 425°F/220°C/Gas Mk 7. Sift the flour, baking powder and salt into a bowl. Add the milk and water and mix to a firm dough but do not knead. Divide into two pieces and shape to fit into two greased 1 lb (450 g) loaf tins. Brush the top with a little milk. Bake for 25 minutes. Cool on a wire rack. Eat as soon as possible, as this bread does not keep.

CHEESE AND NUT LOAF
Makes a 1 lb (450 g) loaf

4 oz (110 g) self-raising flour
4 oz (110 g) wholemeal flour
2 tsp baking powder
1 tsp dry mustard
salt & black pepper to taste
3 oz (75 g) soft margarine
2 oz (50 g) mature Cheddar cheese, grated

Preheat the oven to 350°F/180°C/Gas Mk 4. Place all the ingredients in a bowl and mix until thoroughly blended. Turn into a well greased 1 lb (450 g) loaf tin and level the top. Bake for 1 hour until well risen. Leave in the tin for 5 minutes then turn out onto a wire rack to cool.

SELF-RAISING FLOUR BREAD
Makes 1 round loaf

1 lb (450 g) self-raising flour, sifted
1 tsp salt
1 oz (25 g) butter
½ pint (300 ml) milk and water mixed

Preheat the oven to 425°F/220°C/Gas Mk 7. Sift the flour and salt into a bowl. Rub in the butter until the mixture resembles fine bread-crumbs. Mix to a firm dough with the milk and water and knead until smooth. Shape into a round loaf and place on a greased baking tray. Bake in the oven for 35 minutes and cool on a wire rack. Eat as soon as possible, as this bread does not keep.

GARLIC BREAD
Makes 12 slices

1 French stick
3 oz (75 g) butter
2 cloves of garlic, crushed with a little salt

Preheat the oven to 400°F/200°C/Gas Mk 6. Cut the bread into thick slices, but do not cut through the base of the loaf. Cream together the butter and garlic. Spread this mixture on the bread slices and also spread garlic butter over the crust of the loaf. Wrap in foil and heat in the oven for 10–15 minutes. Cut through the base of each slice and serve immediately.

CHEESE BREAD
Makes 2 x 1 lb (450 g) loaves

1 lb (450 g) plain white flour, sifted
1 tsp salt
1 tsp mustard powder
¼ tsp white pepper
4 oz (110 g) Cheddar cheese, grated
½ oz (15 g) fresh yeast
1 tsp sugar
½ pint (300 ml) warm water

Sift the flour, salt, mustard powder and pepper into a bowl. Stir in the cheese, reserving 1 tbsp. Mix the yeast with the sugar and add to the warm water. Stir into the flour and knead well. Put in an oiled plastic bag and leave to stand for 1 hour. Knead the dough one more time and shape to fit two greased 1 lb (450 g) loaf tins. Cover and leave to stand for 20 minutes. Preheat the oven to 375°F/190°C/Gas Mk 5. Sprinkle the reserved cheese over each loaf and bake for 40 minutes. Cool on a wire rack.

BREAD WITH CARAWAY SEEDS
Makes 2 round loaves

1 lb (450 g) strong white flour, sifted
½ tsp salt
1 oz (25 g) lard
2 tsp caraway seeds
½ oz (15 g) fresh yeast
1 tsp brown sugar
½ pt (300 ml) tepid water

Sift the flour into a bowl and add the salt. Rub in the lard, then stir in the caraway seeds. Mix the fresh yeast with the sugar and add to the warm water. Add the yeast liquid to the flour mixture and mix to a dough. Knead well, put in an oiled plastic bag and leave to stand for 1 hour. Knead the dough again and form into two round shapes. Place on greased baking trays, cover with a tea towel or oiled clingfilm and leave to stand for 45 minutes. Preheat the oven to 400°F/200°C/ Gas Mk 6 and bake for 40 minutes. Cool on a wire rack.

OAT LOAF
Makes a 1 lb (450 g) loaf

10 oz (300 g) strong white flour, sifted
6 oz (175 g) porridge oats
1 tsp salt
1 tsp sugar
½ oz (15 g) fresh yeast or 1½ tsp dried yeast
½ pint (300 ml) warm milk and water mixed
2 tsp sunflower or corn oil
2 tbsp milk
oats, for topping

Sift the flour into a bowl. Add the oats, salt and sugar and stir until well mixed. Place the yeast and milk and water liquid in another bowl and leave until frothy. Then mix the yeast mixture into the flour and add the oil to make a soft dough. Knead well, cover and leave in a warm place for 1 hour. Knead again and divide the dough into three pieces. Roll out the pieces into sausage shapes and plait together loosely. Place on a greased baking sheet, cover and leave for 30 minutes. Preheat the oven to 400°F/200°C/Gas Mk 6. Brush the top of the loaf with a little milk and sprinkle with oats. Bake for 30 minutes. Turn out onto a wire rack to cool.

YOGHURT BREAD
Makes a 1 lb (450 g) loaf

1 lb (450 g) plain wholemeal flour, sifted
4 tsp baking powder
2 tsp light soft brown sugar
1 tsp salt
¼ pint (150 ml) natural yoghurt
¼ pint (150 ml) water

Preheat the oven to 425°F/220°C/Gas Mk 7. Mix the flour, baking powder, sugar and salt together in a bowl. Add the yoghurt and enough water to make a soft dough. Knead well and shape to fit a greased 1 lb (450 g) loaf tin. Bake in the oven for 45 minutes and cool on a wire rack.

ONION BREAD
Makes 1 large round loaf

12 oz (350 g) strong white flour
1 tsp salt
pinch cayenne pepper
1 oz (25 g) margarine
½ oz (15 g) fresh yeast
  or 1½ tsp dried yeast

7 fl oz (200 ml) warm milk
1 tsp sugar
6 oz (175 g) onions, sliced
1 tbsp oil
1 egg, beaten

Sift the flour, salt and cayenne together into a bowl and leave in a warm place for about 5 minutes. Rub in the margarine until the mixture resembles fine breadcrumbs. Crumble the fresh yeast into the warm milk and stir well. If using dried yeast, mix the sugar with a little of the warm milk and sprinkle the yeast on top. Leave in a warm place for about 15 minutes until frothy. Make a well in the flour and pour in the yeast and milk mixture, bringing the flour in from the sides to make a soft dough. Turn onto a lightly floured board and knead for about 10 minutes until smooth. Place the dough in a lightly oiled plastic bag and leave in a warm place for about 1 hour or until doubled in size. Turn the dough onto a floured board and knead again until smooth. Shape into a large ball and place on a greased baking sheet. Flatten the dough on top and make three cuts across the top with a sharp knife. Cover loosely and leave in a warm place for about 30 minutes, or until doubled in size. Preheat the oven to 400°F/200°C/Gas Mk 6. Fry the onions in the oil until soft, but not brown. Drain on kitchen paper. Brush the loaf with beaten egg and spoon the onions on top, pressing them down onto the loaf. Bake for 30–35 minutes, or until the onions are golden and the loaf sounds hollow when tapped on the base. Cover the loaf with foil during cooking if the onions are becoming too brown. Cool on a wire rack.

OATMEAL BREAD
Makes a 2 lb (1 kg) loaf

8 oz (225 g) plain wholemeal
  flour, sifted
6 oz (175 g) coarse oatmeal
2 tsp cream of tartar

1 tsp bicarbonate of soda
1 tsp salt
½ pint (300 ml) milk and
  water mixed

Preheat the oven to 425°F/220°C/Gas Mk 7. Grease a 2 lb (1 kg) loaf tin. Sift the flour into a bowl, add the oatmeal, cream of tartar, soda and salt, and mix thoroughly. Add sufficient milk and water to make a firm dough. Turn into the tin. Bake for 25 minutes. Leave to stand for 5 minutes, then cool on a wire rack.

SAUSAGE BRIOCHE
Makes 6-8 portions

12 oz (350 g) strong plain flour
½ tsp salt
1½ oz (40 g) margarine
1 oz (25 g) caster sugar
1½ tsp dried yeast

8 tbsp warm milk
1 egg, beaten
(225 g) German sausage
  (Knackwurst)

Topping:
1 egg, beaten
1 tsp poppy seeds

Sift the flour into a bowl, add the salt, and rub in the margarine until the mixture resembles fine breadcrumbs. Stir in the sugar and yeast and gradually add the milk. Add the egg and beat to a soft dough. Turn onto a floured board and knead for about 10 minutes, or until smooth. Roll out the dough to a rectangle large enough to wrap around the sausage. Skin the sausage and place in the centre of the dough. Brush the edges of the dough with water and wrap around the sausage, pressing the edges firmly to seal. Place seam side down on a greased baking tray and put this inside a large oiled plastic bag. Leave to rise for about 1 hour or until doubled in size. Preheat the oven to 400°F/200°C/Gas Mk 6. Slash the top of the loaf with a sharp knife about five times, brush with beaten egg and sprinkle with poppy seeds. Bake for 20–25 minutes until golden. Cool on a wire rack. Eat hot or cold.

CELERY BREAD
Makes 8 triangles

1 egg
½ pt (300 ml) water
1 packet celery soup
1 lb (450 g) self-raising flour

1 tsp salt
3 oz (75 g) margarine
a little milk

Preheat the oven to 400°F/200°C/Gas Mk 6. Mix the egg and water in a bowl. Stir in the dry celery soup mix and leave to stand for 10 minutes. Sift the flour into another bowl, add the salt, and rub in the margarine until the mixture resembles fine breadcrumbs. Pour in the soup mixture and mix well. Knead into a round shape, place on a greased baking tray, flatten slightly and brush with a little milk. Lightly score the top into eight wedges and bake in the oven for 35–40 minutes. Serve at once.

HERB BREAD
Makes 2 x 1 lb (450 g) loaves

8 oz (225 g) wholewheat flour
8 oz (225 g) plain flour
2 tsp margarine
1 tsp salt
1 tsp sugar
½ tsp dried dill weed

1 tsp each of dill seed and
dried savoury
2 tsp fresh yeast
10 fl oz (300 ml) warm water
cracked wheat for decoration

Sift the two flours into a large bowl. Rub in the margarine, then add the salt, sugar and dried herbs. Mix together the yeast and water and add to the flour mixture. Mix to a soft dough and knead on a lightly floured surface. Grease two 1 lb (450 g) loaf tins and sprinkle cracked wheat evenly over the bases of the tins. Half fill each tin with the dough. Cover with lightly oiled cling film and set aside in a warm place until the dough has risen and doubled in size. Preheat the oven to 450°F/230°C/Gas Mk 8. Remove cling film and bake for 35 minutes. Serve warm.

CHOLLAH
Makes 1 loaf

1 oz (25 g) fresh yeast
¼ tsp saffron
8 fl oz (225 ml) lukewarm water
1 lb (450 g) strong plain flour

½ tsp salt
1 tsp sugar
2 eggs, beaten
1 egg yolk

Mix the yeast and the saffron with the water and leave to stand for 5 minutes. Sift the flour and mix with the salt and sugar. Mix the yeast liquid with 6 oz (175 g) of the flour mixture, stirring until smooth. Cover with a cloth and leave in a warm place for 30 minutes until the mixture has doubled in size. Add the beaten eggs and mix well. Add the remaining flour and knead the mixture until the dough is smooth. Put the dough in a bowl, dust with a little flour and cover with a cloth. Leave in a warm place for about 2 hours until the dough has doubled in size again. Knead for 5 minutes and divide into 3 equal pieces. Roll these into long round strips and plait them together, tucking in the ends. Put on a greased baking sheet, cover and leave to rise for 1 hour. Preheat the oven to 400°F/200°C/Gas Mk 6. Brush the loaf with egg yolk and bake in the oven for 10 minutes, then reduce the heat to 375°F/190°C/Gas Mark 5 and bake for a further 35 minutes.

CHAPATTIS
Makes 8

8 oz (225 g) wholemeal flour, sifted
large pinch of salt
1 oz (25 g) butter
5 fl oz (150 ml) water
1 tbsp corn oil

Mix the flour and salt in a bowl. Rub in the butter until the mixture resembles fine breadcrumbs. Mix in the water to form a stiff dough. Knead on a lightly floured board for 10 minutes. Leave the dough on the board, cover and leave to rest for 30 minutes. Divide the dough into eight pieces and roll out each piece into a 6 inch (15 cm) circle. Heat the oil in a frying pan and fry each chapatti for 3 minutes, turning frequently. Serve warm.

NAAN BREAD
Makes 12

½ tsp dried yeast
2 tbsp warm water
1½ lb (675 g) self-raising flour
¾ pint (450 ml) natural yoghurt
pinch of salt
2 oz (50 g) melted butter

Stir the yeast into the water and leave for 5 minutes until it starts to bubble. Put the flour in a bowl and work in the yoghurt, salt and yeast liquid. Mix well and knead lightly. Cover with a damp cloth and leave to stand in a warm place for 24 hours. Divide the dough into twelve equal pieces. On a lightly floured board, roll each piece into an oval about ¼ inch (6 mm) thick. Put the pieces on a greased baking sheet. Brush with melted butter and grill for 2 minutes under high heat until brown. Serve warm. The bread should be flat and soft, moist inside and slightly scorched on the outside.

CHEESECAKES AND GATEAUX

CHEESECAKES
Makes 14

6 oz (175 g) plain flour, sifted
pinch of salt

1½ oz (40 g) margarine
1½ oz (40 g) lard

Filling:
raspberry jam
2 oz (50 g) soft margarine
2 oz (50 g) caster sugar
1 large egg
2 oz (50 g) self-raising flour, sifted

finely grated rind of ½ lemon
3 tsp milk
4 glacé cherries, washed, dried
    and quartered

Preheat the oven to 375°F/190°C/Gas Mk 5. Sift the plain flour and salt into a bowl and rub in the margarine and lard until the mixture resembles fine breadcrumbs. Add enough cold water to make a fairly stiff dough. Roll out thinly on a floured board and cut out fourteen 2½ inch (6.5 cm) diameter rounds. Press them into the bases of tartlet tins, reserving the pastry trimmings. To make the filling, put the soft margarine, sugar, egg, sifted flour, lemon rind and milk into a mixing bowl and beat well together for at least 1 minute. Put a spoonful of jam into the base of each pastry tart and spread a spoonful of the creamed mixture on top. Cut the pastry trimmings into thin strips and lay a twist of pastry on top of each tart. Bake in the centre of the oven for 20–25 minutes or until they are well risen and golden brown in colour. Cool on a wire tray.

GINGER AND LEMON ROLL
Serves 4

6 fl oz (175 ml) double cream
4 oz (110 g) Greek yoghurt
2 tsp clear honey

grated rind of ½ lemon
14 ginger nut biscuits
2 pieces stem ginger, finely sliced

Lightly whip the cream until it holds its shape. Stir the honey and lemon rind into the yoghurt and fold this into the cream. Sandwich the biscuits into a roll using two-thirds of the cream mixture, and place on a shallow serving dish or plate. Smooth half the remaining cream mixture over the outside of the roll and pipe the remaining cream along the top. Decorate with the slices of stem ginger. Chill.

BAKED CHEESECAKE
Serves 6

Base:
8 oz (225 g) digestive biscuits
2 level tsp caster sugar
4 oz (110 g) butter, melted

Filling:
½ pint (300 ml) milk
1 tbsp lemon juice
4 eggs
5 oz (150 g) caster sugar

2 level tbsp flour
¼ level tsp salt
1 lb (450 g) cottage cheese
icing sugar, for dusting

Preheat the oven to 325°F/170°C/Gas Mk 3. Lightly grease an 8 inch (20 cm) round loose-based spring-form cake tin. Finely crumble the biscuits, mix with the sugar and mix into the melted butter. Press half of this mixture into the base of the tin. Put the remaining ingredients, with the exception of the icing sugar and remaining half of the biscuit mixture, into a blender and mix thoroughly. Pour this mixture over the crumb base. Bake for 1–1¼ hours or until the centre is firm. Cool completely and then cover carefully with the rest of the crumb mixture. Cut six strips of greaseproof paper, 1 inch (2.5 cm) wide, and use to make a lattice pattern over the top layer of the biscuit mixture. Dust with icing sugar and then carefully remove the paper strips.

AUSTRIAN COFFEE CAKE
Serves 6–8

6 oz (175 g) margarine
6 oz (175 g) caster sugar
3 eggs, size 3
6 oz (175 g) self-raising flour, sifted
pinch of salt

4 level tbsp coffee essence
1 level tbsp dark brown sugar
½ pint (300 ml) boiling water
2 tbsp rum

Preheat the oven to 375°F/190°C/Gas Mk 5. Grease a 1½ pint (1 litre) ring mould. Cream the margarine and caster sugar together until light and fluffy. Add the eggs, one at a time, beating well after each addition. Fold in the sifted flour and salt. Spoon the mixture into the mould and level the top. Bake in the oven for 30 minutes until springy to the touch. Leave to cool in the tin for 5 minutes, then turn out onto a wire rack. Blend the coffee essence with the brown sugar, water and rum and leave to cool. Stand the cake on a large plate and slowly pour over the coffee liquid, making sure that all the cake surface is moistened. Leave for 2 hours to soak up the coffee liquid.

YOGHURT CHEESECAKE
Makes an 8 inch (20 cm) cake

3 oz (75 g) butter
4 oz (110 g) biscuits (digestive),
  crumbed
3 tsp gelatine
4 fl oz (125 ml) cold water
1 lb (450 g) cottage cheese
8 fl oz (225 ml) yoghurt
4 eggs, separated

14 oz (400 g) caster sugar
1 tbsp lemon rind
¼ pt (150 ml) whipping cream
1 jar or can black cherries, drained
  (reserve the juice)
1 packet red jelly
¼ pt (150 ml) boiling water

Melt the butter gently and mix with the biscuit crumbs. Press into a deep 8 inch (20 cm) loose-bottomed cake tin and chill. Soften the gelatine in the cold water. Press the cottage cheese through a sieve and beat it with the yoghurt until smooth. In a bowl over a pan of gently simmering water beat the egg yolks with 6 oz (175 g) sugar and the lemon rind until the mixture is thick and creamy. Add the softened gelatine and stir until this has dissolved. Remove from the heat and cool slightly. Stir in the yoghurt–cheese mixture. Whisk the egg whites in a clean, dry bowl until they form stiff peaks and gradually add the remaining sugar to make a meringue. Fold in the lemon mixture, and then the softly whipped cream. Pour carefully onto the crumb base. Chill in the refrigerator until set. Strain the cherries and reserve ½ pint (300 ml) of the juice. Dissolve the jelly in boiling water and add the cherry juice. Place in the refrigerator until it is beginning to set. Arrange the cherries on top of the cheesecake, carefully spoon the jelly over the cherries and refrigerate overnight.

AUSTRIAN CURD CAKE
Serves 6

12 oz (350 g) cottage cheese
2½ oz (65 g) butter
5 oz (150 g) caster sugar
2 eggs, separated
3 oz (75 g) raisins

1 oz (25 g) ground almonds
2 tbsp semolina
juice of 1 medium lemon
grated rind of ½ medium lemon
sifted icing sugar for dusting

Preheat the oven to 375°F/190°C/Gas Mk 5. Sieve the cheese. Cream the butter with the sugar, then gradually beat in the cheese and egg yolks. Blend in the raisins, almonds, semolina, lemon rind and lemon juice. Beat the egg whites until stiff, then lightly fold into the creamed mixture. Spoon into a greased and lined 7 inch (18 cm) sandwich tin. Bake in the oven for 1 hour or until golden brown. Cool in the tin, then remove and dust with sifted icing sugar.

FRUIT CHEESECAKE
Makes an 8 inch (20 cm) cake

½ oz (15 g) semi-sweet biscuit crumbs
12 oz–1 lb (350–450 g) cottage cheese
2 oz (50 g) butter
4 oz (110 g) caster sugar
4 eggs, separated
2 tbsp stiffly whipped cream
2 tbsp cornflour
2 tbsp lemon juice
1 tsp finely grated rind of 1 lemon

Preheat the oven to 350°F/180°C/Gas Mk 4. Grease an 8 inch (20 cm) loose-bottomed cake tin and sprinkle with the biscuit crumbs. Cream together the butter and sugar, then gradually beat in the egg yolks. Add the cream, cornflour, lemon juice and lemon rind and mix thoroughly. Sieve the cottage cheese into the mixture, mixing well. Stiffly whisk the egg whites and fold into the mixture. Pile into the cake tin and bake in the oven for 1½ hours. Leave to cool slightly before removing from the tin.

COFFEE WALNUT DESSERT GATEAU
Serves 6–8

1 level tbsp instant coffee powder
5 oz (150 g) unsalted butter
3 oz (75 g) icing sugar
3 egg yolks
24 boudoir (or sponge finger) biscuits
¼ pt (150 ml) cold strong black coffee
coffee liqueur (optional)
1 oz (25 g) walnut halves
whipped cream (optional)

NB: This cake must be made a day in advance, as it needs 24 hours to set.

Dissolve the instant coffee powder in 3 tsp boiling water. Cream the butter and icing sugar. Beat the egg yolks, then gradually beat them into the creamed mixture. Stir in the dissolved coffee. Place eight of the biscuits side by side on a plate and sprinkle over them 3–4 tbsp of the cold black coffee. (1 tbsp of the coffee mixture can be replaced by 1 tbsp of coffee liqueur on this and each of the other layers.) Spread one third of the coffee butter cream over the biscuits. Arrange two rows of biscuits (four to each row) at right angles on top of the first layer, sprinkle over 3–4 tbsp coffee and then coat the biscuits with another third of the coffee butter cream. Arrange a final layer of eight biscuits side by side on top and sprinkle with coffee as before. Spread the remaining coffee butter cream on top. Leave the cake in a cool place for 24 hours so that the coffee soaks through and gives the gateau the desired texture. Decorate the top with walnut halves, and whipped cream, if desired.

LINZERTORTE

6 oz (175 g) soft margarine
2 oz (50 g) caster sugar
2 oz (50 g) ground hazelnuts
grated rind of 1 lemon
1 egg, beaten
8 oz (225 g) plain flour

½ tsp ground cinnamon
1 lb (450 g) raspberries or
  raspberry jam
2 tbsp redcurrant jelly
icing sugar for dusting

Preheat the oven to 375°F/190°C/Gas Mk 5. Put the margarine, sugar, ground nuts, lemon rind, egg and 1 oz (25 g) flour in a bowl. Cream with a fork until the ingredients are thoroughly mixed. Work in the remaining flour and the cinnamon to form a soft dough. Turn onto a lightly floured board and work until smooth. The dough is very delicate and must be handled carefully. Roll out two-thirds of the dough to line an 8 inch (20 cm) flan ring placed on a baking sheet. Chill for 30 minutes. Fill the pastry case with raspberry jam or with the raspberries which have been lightly stewed in their own juice and sweetened to taste. Roll out the remaining dough and cut into ½ inch (1.25 cm) strips. Arrange these in a lattice pattern on top of the raspberries or jam. Bake in the oven for 35 minutes. Cool, then brush the lattice and the edge of the pastry with melted redcurrant jelly. Dust with icing sugar.

FRUIT AND CURD CHEESE CAKE
Serves 6

1 lb (450 g) curd cheese
2 oz (50 g) cornflour
grated rind of 1 lemon
6 dessertspoons sugar
4 oz (110 g) butter, melted
4 fl oz (125 ml) natural yoghurt
6 eggs, beaten
2 oz (50 g) currants, soaked in hot water
7 oz (200 g) whole preserved fruit, drained and chopped

In a mixing bowl, blend together the curd cheese, cornflour, lemon rind, sugar and melted butter. Add the yoghurt, beaten eggs, drained soaked currants and chopped fruit. Pour the mixture into a greased cake tin and bake in the oven at 350°F/180°C/Gas Mk 4 for 30 minutes until set.

TIPSY APPLE GATEAU

¾ pint (450 ml) sweet cider
5 oz (150 g) granulated sugar
4 oz (110 g) seedless raisins
3 eggs

3 oz (75 g) caster sugar
2½ oz (65 g) plain flour
1 cooking apple
¼ pint (150 ml) double cream

Preheat the oven to 375°F/190°C/Gas Mk 5. Put ½ pint (300 ml) cider, 4 oz (110 g) granulated sugar and the raisins in a saucepan. Bring to the boil and reduce the liquid by half. Cool, cover and leave to stand overnight. Whisk the eggs and caster sugar until thick in a bowl placed over a saucepan of simmering water. Remove from the heat and continue to whisk until the mixture has cooled. Fold in the sifted flour, a little at a time. Turn into two greased 7 inch (17.5 cm) sandwich tins and bake in the oven for 15 minutes. Leave to cool in the tins for 5 minutes before turning out onto wire racks. Drain the raisins, reserving the syrup. Peel, core and slice the apple, and poach it very gently in the remaining cider and granulated sugar until just tender. Drain and cool. Whip the cream stiffly. Brush one of the cake layers with the reserved raisin syrup, then spread over half the whipped cream and cover with the raisins. Put the other cake on top, brush with the raisin syrup (reserving 2 tbsp). Arrange the poached apple slices on top. Brush with the remaining syrup and decorate with the remaining whipped cream.

QUICK CHEESECAKES
Serves 4

8 oz (225 g) strawberries or raspberries
8 oz (225 g) full-fat soft cheese
2 oz (50 g) icing sugar

4 digestive biscuits
double or whipping cream to
garnish

Reserve four whole fruit and chop the remainder finely. Beat the cheese and icing sugar together and mix in the chopped fruit. Butter and base line four individual ramekin dishes and spoon the cheese and fruit mixture evenly into these. Place one digestive biscuit on top of each. Chill in the refrigerator for at least 1 hour. With a thin sharp knife ease the cheesecakes away from the sides of the ramekins and tip them out onto individual serving plates. Carefully remove the lining and garnish with a swirl of whipped cream and a whole fruit on top of each cake.

INDEX

Abernethy biscuits *143*
Afghans *96*
Almond and cherry cake with sherry *6*
Almond and cherry slices *77*
Almond apricot tart *83*
Almond cake *23*
Almond cookies *106*
Almond crisps *90*
Almond crunchies *125*
Almond jumblies *119*
Almond macaroons *101*
Almond squares *77*
Almond tart *87*
Amaretti biscuits *100*
American muffins *65*
Anzacs *94*
Apple and marzipan tart *72*
Apple and nut bread *153*
Apple cider cake *19*
Apple crumble cake *9*
Apple slice *84*
Apple strudel *86*
Apricot and prune loaf *167*
Apricot and walnut loaf *164*
Apricot oat crunchies *91*
Apricot upside-down cake *29*
Aunt Belle's parkin *43*
Austrian coffee cake *184*
Austrian curd cake *185*

Bacon and seed scones *67*
Baked cheesecake *184*
Baking powder bread *175*
Banana and date bread *160*
Banana bread *156*
Banana rock cakes *55*
Banana upside-down cake *31*
Banana yoghurt cake *12*
Banbury cakes 1 *81*
Banbury cakes 2 *82*
Bara brith *161*
Barley bannocks *63*
Betty's brownies *57*
Boozy bake *28*
Boozy fruit and nut clusters *113*
Bosworth jumbles *126*
Bourbon biscuits *97*
Brack bread *168*

Bran bundles *109*
Bran scones *67*
Bread with caraway seeds *177*
Brioches *171*
Butterfly cakes *27*
Butternut wafers *132*
Butterscotch cake *24*

California crunchies *109*
Caramel glory cake *18*
Caraway cookies *131*
Carrot and date cake *16*
Celery bread *180*
Chapattis *182*
Cheese and herb bread *173*
Cheese and nut loaf *176*
Cheese bread *177*
Cheese crackers *144*
Cheese scones *63*
Cheese straws *135*
Cheesecakes *183*
Chequerboard cake *44*
Cherry and banana bread *164*
Cherry and date cake *12*
Cherry and nut cookies *117*
Cherry cake *11*
Cherry cakes *27*
Cherry marshmallow bars *54*
Cherry oat biscuits *148*
Cherry rounds *108*
Choc and cherry biscuits *95*
Chocoholic's delight *39*
Chocolate and raisin drops *110*
Chocolate biscuits *130*
Chocolate brandy cake *41*
Chocolate cake *26*
Chocolate chip cookies *104*
Chocolate cream fingers *98*
Chocolate crispies *129*
Chocolate cup cakes *26*
Chocolate fudge cake *45*
Chocolate kisses *99*
Chocolate layer squares *38*
Chocolate macaroons *97*
Chocolate madeleines *28*
Chocolate meringues *59*
Chocolate mountains *115*
Chocolate oil cake *34*

Chocolate peppermint cream cookies 92
Chocolate polka dot cake 42
Chocolate ring biscuits 126
Chocolate topped orange loaf 158
Chocolate Viennese slices 121
Chollah 181
Chopped peanut loaf 156
Cider bread 151
Cinnamon cherry bars 53
Cinnamon cookies 105
Cinnamon crispies 130
Cinnamon drop scones 62
Cinnamon lemon biscuits 140
Cinnamon loaf 166
Cinnamon plum tart 78
Cinnamon twists 75
Citrus biscuits 122
Coconut and cherry biscuits 133
Coconut and lemon pyramids 149
Coconut biscuits 137
Coconut bread 169
Coconut cake 35
Coconut cookies 95
Coconut kisses 56
Coconut macaroons 113
Coconut shortbread 139
Coffee and walnut cake 26
Coffee crescents 136
Coffee fudge squares 85
Coffee walnut biscuits 94
Coffee walnut dessert gateau 186
Cornbread 1 174
Cornbread 2 174
Cornflake crunchies 50
Cornish fairings 125
Cottage cheese and fruit teabread 154
Cottage cheese drop scones 61
Country nut loaf 157
Cracknell biscuits 138
Cream crackers 134
Crispy date triangles 49
Crumbly chocolate squares 58
Crunchy fingers 143
Curd tart 88
Curried cheese biscuits 144

Danish brown biscuits 93
Danish delights 108
Danish love rings 60
Date and orange tart 76
Date and walnut loaf 1 159
Date and walnut loaf 2 159
Date bread 155

Date crunchies 51
Date triangles 72
De luxe cookies 107
Digestives 115
Double chocolate biscuits 123
Drop scones 64
Dundee cake 10
Dutch honey and spice loaf 165
Dutch kisses 145

Easter biscuits 138
Easy tea bread 161
Eccles cakes 58
Exotic fruit rock cakes 59

Fig cookies 89
Flapjacks 52
Freda's macaroons 142
Frosted coffee marble cake 34
Fruit and curd cheese cake 187
Fruit cheesecake 186
Fudge brownies 56
Funny face cookies 111

Garibaldi biscuits 117
Garlic bread 176
Genoese sponge 33
Georgian gingerbreads 110
German biscuits 132
German coffee cake 33
Giant rum and raisin ranch cookies 103
Ginger and lemon roll 183
Ginger sponge cake 26
Ginger cake 35
Ginger crisps 112
Ginger crunchies 124
Ginger flapjacks 53
Ginger melting moments 102
Ginger nuts 128
Ginger whirls 52
Ginger-flavoured cheese bars 55
Gingerbread 170
Gingered peanut loaf 155
Golden sponge 39
Gooseberry almond tart 80
Grandma's gingerbread 37
Granny loaf 172
Granny's rock cakes 46
Grantham gingerbreads 119
Greek yoghurt cake 15
Guinness cake 8

Half pound cake *10*
Hazelnut squares *147*
Herb bread *181*
Honey flapjacks *127*
Honey fruit bread *154*
Hot apple scones *64*
Hungarian biscuits *140*

Iced cherry cakes *46*
Iced ginger oaties *134*
Iced raisin cookies *147*
Irish bannock *66*
Irish treacle loaf *163*
Italian crisp macaroons *146*

Jack Horner cake *7*
Jam sandwich biscuits *137*
Jamaican tea loaf *167*
Jeannie's Bakewell tart *78*
John Peel cake *17*

Kids' delight *106*

Lardy cake *23*
Lemon and almond cake *22*
Lemon and honey sponge layer slices *50*
Lemon and lime cookies *141*
Lemon and orange cookies *121*
Lemon cake *27*
Lemon curd crunchies *133*
Lemon custard tarts *69*
Lemon fingers *74*
Lemon puffs *83*
Lemon shortbread *146*
Light fruit cake *21*
Linzertorte *187*

Macaroons *150*
Madeira cake *32*
Madeleines *49*
Malt loaf *165*
Malted fruit bread *152*
Maple walnut biscuits *93*
Marble biscuits *136*
Marble cake *30*
Marmalade cake *29*
Marmalade chews *99*
Marmalade tea bread *169*
Marzipan puffs *71*
Melting moments *100*
Midas macaroons *141*
Mincemeat slices *79*
Mocha cake *37*

Mocha cookies *149*
Muesli cookies *104*
Muesli loaf *162*
Mum's favourite *20*
Mum's parkin *40*

Naan bread *182*
Nut cookies *118*
Nutty bread *153*
Nutty honey bunches *112*

Oat and almond biscuits *130*
Oat crunchies *124*
Oat loaf *178*
Oatmeal bread *179*
Oaty biscuits *128*
Old-fashioned seed cake *36*
Old-fashioned sultana cake *16*
Onion bread *179*
Orange and coconut flapjacks *48*
Orange and ginger cookies *129*
Orange and walnut loaf *157*
Orange bread *170*
Orange cake *27*
Orange chocolate slices *48*
Orange honey cake *14*
Orange meringue bars *57*
Orange tart *73*
Orange treacle loaf *168*

Palmiers *70*
Peach and hazelnut delight *18*
Peanut butter cookies *114*
Peanut crackers *107*
Peanut oaties *127*
Pear and nut cake *15*
Peppernut biscuits *98*
Pikelets *61*
Pineapple and raisin bread *160*
Pineapple bread *152*
Pineapple cake *6*
Pineapple upside-down cake *30*
Plain buns *65*
Polish walnut cake *22*
Polka dot cake *28*
Potato bread *173*
Potato scones *66*
Pumpkin cake *13*

Queen cakes *52*
Quick cheesecakes *188*
Quick cherry almond cake *14*

Raisin and banana bakes *111*
Raisin and peanut scones *68*
Raspberry rounds *51*
Rhubarb bake *86*
Ribbon biscuits *123*
Ribbon layer cake *40*
Rich fruit cake *8*
Rolled oat cookies *103*
Rum cake *43*

Sausage brioche *180*
Savoury oatmeal biscuits *118*
Seed cake *7*
Self-raising flour bread *176*
Semi-sweet oatmeal biscuits *92*
Sesame cookies *89*
Sesame seed cake *19*
Shell biscuits *148*
Shortbread *142*
Shortie digestive biscuits *145*
Shrewsbury biscuits *116*
Shrewsbury currant biscuits *120*
Sly cakes *82*
Snow white cake *36*
Soda bread *175*
Speculatius *122*
Spice biscuits *90*
Spiced bread *162*
Spicy Christmas cookies *116*
Spicy date cake *9*
Spicy honey cake *42*
Spotted Dick cake *28*
Springerle *139*
Sticky ginger madeleines *47*
Sticky nut pie *70*
Strawberry buns *47*
Strawberry puffs *76*
Sugary rings *91*
Sultana squares *75*
Summer fruit tarts *79*
Sunflower crispies *118*
Sweet drop scones *61*
Swiss tarts *54*
Syrup and nut bread *163*
Syrupy yoghurt cake *31*

Tipsy apple gateau *188*
Toffee shortcake *73*
Treacle biscuits *128*
Treacle drop scones *65*
Treacle loaf *151*
Tuiles *102*
Turkish halva cake *32*

Upside-down plum cake *11*

Vanilla biscuits *105*
Vanilla butter biscuits *131*
Vanilla snaps *120*
Vanilla square *41*
Victoria sponge 1 *25*
Victoria sponge 2 *25*
Viennese tarts *74*

Walnut and choc chip cookies *114*
Walnut cake *20*
Walnut kisses *58*
Walnut loaf *166*
Walnut spice fingers *132*
Walnut squares *84*
Walnut tart *71*
Welsh cakes *62*
Welsh currant loaf *158*
White buttons *135*
Wholemeal fruit scones *60*
Wholemeal scones *68*
Wholewheat shorties *96*
Wine biscuits *101*

Yoghurt bread *178*
Yoghurt cheesecake *185*
Yoghurt drop scones *66*
Yorkshire parkin *17*